A Girl and Five

By Sonora Carver

As Told To Elizabeth Land

ISBN: 978-1-63923-521-6

Printed: October 2022

Cover Art By: Amit Paul

Published and Distributed By:
Lushena Books
607 Country Club Drive, Unit E
Bensenville, IL 60106
www.lushenabks.com

ISBN: 978-1-63923-521-6

To Al

One

As I sat in the grandstand at the fairgrounds that night in 1923 I had no idea that less than a year from that time I would be performing the act I was about to witness. Nothing in my background had prepared me to expect it, nor had any personal inclination led me toward it, and yet what was about to happen was to change my entire life.

In front of the grandstand was a broad green stretch of ground on which different kinds of equipment—high wires, trapezes, and the like—had been set up for various acts. But by far the most impressive was a tall tower that stood to the left. It was freshly painted white and so enormous it dwarfed everything else in sight.

A girl in a red bathing suit, brown football helmet, and white sneakers sat on a railing at the top of the tower, looking intently down a steep ramp. In a moment she gave a signal with her hand and instantly there came the sound of a horse's hoofs hitting the runway. Streamers of lights on the tower quivered and braces and supports vibrated as the horse galloped up, and then, as if by magic, the horse's forequarters appeared. She came off the ramp onto an aisle that led to the front of the tower, and as she galloped past the girl on the railing the girl jumped on.

They drew up together at the head of the platform, where there was a sheer drop-off, and the horse stood for a moment like a beautiful statue, looking down at the audience in the grandstand and at a tank of water that lay in front of the tower.

To my everlasting memory I saw she was dapple-gray, her forequarters wholly white, her flanks heavily marbled with gray. She had a white mane, which was flung to one side, and a white tail like a plume to the flow, and she looked as proud as any duchess, yet full of strength and power. I might have guessed, had I not already known, that her name was the Duchess of Lightning.

I, who had loved horses since I was old enough to know what they were, was completely spellbound. I thought she was the most beautiful animal I had ever seen in my life or was ever likely to see.

After looking the crowd over to her satisfaction she slid her forefeet down. A series of planks, set one beside the other, was nailed flat to the front of the platform, and it was here she braced herself. She hung for a moment at an almost perpendicular angle, then pushed away from the boards and lunged outward into space. For a split second her form was imprinted on the night sky like a silhouette, then her beautiful body arched gracefully over and down and plunged into the tank.

Sheets of water splashed up, hung there bright and crystal-edged, then fell back into the tank, writhing and boiling in the place where they had disappeared. For a moment nothing happened, and then the horse shot up, rocketed from the bottom by her own impetus, but as if catapulted.

The girl was still on her back. The horse swam toward the front of the tank and I noticed her ferocious expression. Her nostrils were sucked in and her teeth were bared, and for a moment I was frightened. Then I realized that nothing was wrong; it was just her way of keeping the water out. After a moment she reached an incline at the front of the tank and cantered out onto dry ground, where the rider slipped off her back.

By this time everyone was clapping and some were shouting and stamping. It was obvious that everyone was as thrilled as I was.

I turned to my date sitting next to me. "Would you do that?" I asked.

He said, "Do you think I'm crazy!"

It was a common enough answer and a sensible one, too, but it had special meaning for me because I had said almost the same thing to my mother three days before. She had come to my room at the boardinghouse on one of her odder missions; she wanted me to go with her to the Savannah Hotel to see the people who were presenting the diving-horse act at the fair.

"Why should I want to meet them?" I asked in astonishment.

"Because they're looking for someone to dive the horses, and you'd be perfect for it."

"Me!" I said. "Dive on a horse? Mother, you've lost your mind!"

"No," she said, "I haven't. You've got all the qualifications." And as if to prove it, she handed me a want ad. She had torn it from the paper and the edges were all jagged.

Wanted: Attractive young woman who can swim and dive. Likes horses, desires to travel. See Dr. W. F. Carver, Savannah Hotel.

I handed it back to her with the words, "I'm not interested."

"But don't you see? It offers everything you've ever wanted! And you've got all the qualifications!"

"I don't care," I said. "I'm not interested. Traveling around with a carnival!"

"It's *not* a carnival," she insisted. "They travel by themselves. And what's more, it's one of the finest acts in the country. Everybody says so."

"I don't care," I repeated. "I'm not interested. I don't want to meet them." And the more she argued, the more resistant I became, which is understandable only if you knew Mother.

With Mother a person had to be stubborn to stay sane. Mother hadn't a shred of practicality and was as irresponsible as a cockroach. Completely lacking in organization, she could not be depended on for anything. A person might have called her an eccentric, but of a definite type. She was an undercover eccentric because her eccentricities didn't show. She didn't wear a spider in her hair or an old Confederate overcoat or get up in the night and beat on a frying pan. On the contrary, her eccentricities were hidden beneath a veil of normality, and you had to live with Mother to know. If you did you were sure.

"Now look," I said, "I'm not going down to the hotel with you and that's all there is to it."

"But I *told* them I'd bring you."

"Then you'll have to tell them you were mistaken."

"You're passing up the chance of a lifetime."

"I don't think so," I replied.

That's the way it began, just as simple as that, the way so many things in life begin and end up having the impact of King Kong. For me the most world-shaking event in my life began with nothing more than a mild-mannered want ad read by my mother, for the upshot of the matter was that she wouldn't quit talking about it that day or the next, so that finally I relented. I'd go to the hotel with her, I said, if she'd promise to leave me alone.

It was a Wednesday evening and they were all in the hotel lobby—Dr. Carver, his son Allen, a daughter Lorena, and Vivian, a girl who rode for them. Dr. Carver was, I found, the most distinguished-looking man I had ever met. I didn't admit this to Mother then or later, but I was quite impressed. He was eighty-four years old at the time but didn't look it. He stood tall and straight like a redwood and was apparently as indestructible. His complexion was ruddy, with a series of ridges stamped between his remarkably penetrating eyes. As we talked about the act and the possibility of my joining it, I had the feeling he could see the bones in my skull.

Although he did offer me the job with his company I turned him down, explaining politely that I didn't think it was what I wanted to do and that I had really come along only to placate my mother. I don't remember my exact words, but that was the gist of it, and if I remember correctly he smiled and said something like, "I understand," and after that we left.

Meeting Dr. Carver, however, stimulated my interest if not my appetite, and I was more anxious to see the act than I had been before. Hence I'd gone to the fair with my date and seen the show in which the diving-horse act was the finale. After I had watched the magnificent dapple-gray horse my whole outlook changed. As emphatically as I had not wished to learn to ride a diving horse, I now wished to learn. The fact was that I had fallen in love, simply and completely.

To understand how I felt about horses one should know that when I was only five years old I tried to trade my brother for a horse. When H.S. was six weeks old I willingly would have traded him for a bay named Sam had my parents not objected.

Sam was the carriage horse of the woman who lived next door, and she knew I loved him as I loved nothing else in the world. One day, as a joke, she asked me if I'd trade. I knew good and well I could get a new baby brother practically any time, but a horse! A horse was something else. Would I trade? Of course I would! I raced into the house, snatched H.S. out of his crib, and tore back out with him, afraid that if I didn't hurry she'd change her mind. Just as I was about to hand him over, however, I had the feeling that someone was watching and, when I turned, there were my mother and father standing on the back porch.

I don't think I have ever had a sicker feeling. I knew instantly they didn't want me to trade and nearly burst out crying. As it was, I managed to say, "I'm sorry. I can't." I took him back inside and put him in his bed, literally bursting with grief.

This love of horses was to remain with me for the rest of my life and to lead me into strange acts, some of them nearly catastrophic.

The year I started school I discovered a penful of horses down at the railroad yards. Waycross, Georgia, was a stop-ping-off place for feeding and watering livestock on their way to tie stockyards. Of course they were mostly cattle, but there were some horses, too, and after I found they could be seen every morning I stopped each day on my way to school. As a result I was chronically tardy but I never mended my ways. Even when the teacher threatened to fail me I continued to come in late. I had no use for the first grade and, to make matters worse, entered the room with a savoir-faire that would have felled Sinatra. In the end, however, the teacher had the last word. She flunked me.

That should have taught me a lesson, but I refused to be taught. I carried my truancy with me right on up through high school. As late as the tenth grade I was cutting classes to go horseback riding and once nearly killed our principal. He had the poor sense to cut back through the city park on his way from watching baseball practice and was following the bridle path when I came bouncing along. I pulled aside in time to avoid running him down but not in time to avoid being spotted. The next morning I was called into his office and threatened with expulsion if I cut school again.

He needn't have worried. I quit—not because of a horse, however. My school career ended when my mother was called away to be with Grandfather, who was ill, and left me to take care of the children. She hadn't meant for me to stay home, but that is what I did. The real reason was that I had fallen in love and had been rejected. A rejected eighteen-year-old is like a runaway torpedo. There's no telling what she will do or in which direction she'll go. For me it was the next thing to being thrown from a horse, and I simply couldn't bear it, so I minded the children and stayed out of sight of my classmates.

To reveal the plain foolhardiness of my action, it is necessary to say that the love affair had gone no deeper than a few soulful looks and a couple of Saturday-night movies, but pride is a woeful thing, powerfully strong in me.

How often I've regretted it, it would be impossible to say. The real sorrow is that in spite of everything I had always made good grades, and had I really tried I might have become a student. But there I was out of school, and after a while I went to work. Before this happened, however, Mother moved herself and my five brothers and sisters to Savannah, Georgia. It was an ad that hooked her.

> For Sale: Two acres on Burnside River, fifteen miles from Savannah. Five-room stucco cottage, modern conveniences, two-car garage, boathouse, private pier, six rowboats. Cash or terms.

Mother was addicted to ads. She read them with the avidity of a bird watcher watching a bird, and as a result made some marvelous purchases. Once it was a covey of fish bowls which she set about the house, not because we had a lot of goldfish, but because the bowls were on sale.

Another time it was an office building which she converted into a boardinghouse. Very few people have bedded down in former chiropractic treatment rooms, but her boarders did. Another time she made cosmetics at home to sell to the neighbors. For quite a while after she read that ad we had pestles and mortars around with mysterious mixtures ground up in them and non-edible messes bubbling on the stove.

Mother was clever and could have been quite successful at almost anything if it hadn't been that, once she got a project going, she completely lost interest. She had a mind like a dragonfly, restless and always on the move, and sometimes we moved too. During the years of my growing up it was difficult for me to count the number of houses we had lived in. She would see an ad for a house to rent and decide it had more closet space than ours. In a twinkling we'd find ourselves lugging our belongings halfway across town.

Sometimes, however, she moved without even telling us. One day we came home from school and there wasn't a stick of furniture in the house. A man was sweeping up and told us we had moved, and he also told us where. When we got there we found Mother unpacking dishes. She said yes, we'd moved. So the shift to Savannah was no surprise to me, although I was visiting an aunt in Florida at the time and had had no idea that Mother was thinking of moving. But then, neither had she. Only when she read the want ad had the seizure hit her and she had been struck with the idea of buying the stucco cottage and making a lodge out of it for hunters. She planned to rent rooms to them and give them early-morning breakfast before they went out to hunt. She didn't say any of this in the letter to me, though. She just wrote, "When you come back, don't go to Bainbridge. We don't live there any more."

I was old enough then to have impeded her had I been home, but by the time I got to Savannah it was clearly too late. All the children were out splashing around in the river and everyone was happy. The boathouse proved to be nothing more than a shed, and the fleet of six boats had been whittled down to one buckled and spavined specimen. What was more, the house was so small she couldn't possibly have rented any rooms. There were seven of us and only five rooms any way you counted them.

For my part, after my first trip to town—a five-mile walk to the trolley line, followed by a forty-minute ride—I made up my mind to rent a room in town and get myself a job. Until then the children had been too small for me to leave them, but they would all be in school that fall and I could get out and view the world, which I'd been straining to see ever since I was two years old.

I remember that time quite clearly because it was my running-away period. At least Mother called it "running away." I knew perfectly well that I was coming back. Apparently she wasn't so sure, because after a series of "runaways" she began to lock me in the back yard in order to keep me at home. I soon learned to climb the fence and take off. The situation finally became so critical, she adopted the suggestion of a friend. She put a flour sack over my head and tied it down with string.

The theory behind this was that I'd be so ashamed to be seen looking that way that I'd automatically stay home. However, she reckoned without the determination which came in so handy later. The first time she tried it she found me about an hour later two blocks away playing with some children who, apparently having satisfied themselves that there was a head under the sack, welcomed me into their games.

In all fairness to the plan it should be said that the child was not expected to suffocate. The sacks had been washed and were sleazy enough to be breathed through and seen through without difficulty.

From what has been said it should be apparent that, for all Mother's whimsicalities, she was not entirely mistaken when she thought of me in connection with Dr. Carver's ad. As a matter of fact, she had every good reason to believe I'd make an excellent performer. I *was* young (nineteen), I was attractive (people said so), and I liked to travel (even with sacks on my head). I did love horses (H.S. was still with us but had had a narrow escape) and I could swim and dive.

The night I went home after seeing the act I told Jac, my younger sister, who was living with me and going to school in Savannah, that I had changed my mind. "I want to learn to ride the diving horses," I said. "I'm going to take the job."

"Well, you'd better hurry," she said. "They're leaving tomorrow."

There was a paper lying on the bedroom floor and she pointed to it. I picked it up and read a headline on an inside page.

"CARVER HIGH-DIVING HORSE ACT MOST SUCCESSFUL AT FAIR," and beneath it, "Dr. Carver carved place in old West."

It was a full-page write-up about him and his diving horses, intended to boost attendance at the fair. For me it served the purpose of introducing him to me more thoroughly than anything else could have.

According to the write-up, Dr. Carver had been part of the old West when the West was really wild. Back in the middle 1800s he had acted as scout for a regiment of cavalry stationed near the site of North Platte, Nebraska, although North Platte wasn't yet there. Along with the scouting, he had hunted and trapped and was one of the first men to file papers for a homestead in Frontier County, Nebraska. He might have settled there, he was quoted as saying, had it not been that about that time the commercial demand for leather became so great that anybody who was a good rifleshot got busy killing buffalo. He had seen the time when the skinned carcasses lay so close to one another that a man could walk for miles without touching the ground, just stepping from one body to another. He said that now he regretted the waste of all that meat and the suffering it had caused the Indians by taking their main source of food, but that in those days he had been too young to feel any sense of shame. He was only in his late teens and busy getting rich. Also, he was becoming a deadly shot with a rifle; so deadly, in fact, that he could shoot out the eye of a buffalo while riding at full gallop. The Indians were so frightened of him that they gave him the name of "Evil Spirit."

He was broad-shouldered, six foot four, and weighed 210 pounds. He had flaming red hair and a pair of long mustaches. In the manner of the plainsmen of that day he wore his hair shoulder-length, as did his friends Buffalo Bill Cody and Wild Bill Hickok, with whom he spent much of his time.

When the hide market finally became glutted he decided he wanted to try something else, and since the career of a professional man had a certain appeal for him, he decided to take up dentistry. In order to learn how to pull teeth he had to go to school, the closest one being in California. He decided to go there and persuaded Wild Bill Hickok to go with him, but at the last minute Wild Bill changed his mind because of a gold strike in North Dakota. He tried to sell Dr. Carver on the idea of going to North Dakota, and they ended by flipping a coin to see whether it would be California or North Dakota.

Dr. Carver won the toss, but Wild Bill still refused to go to California. "You'll run into bad luck, Bill," Dr. Carver argued, "if you buck the coin." But Bill bucked it anyway, and the next thing Dr. Carver heard Wild Bill was dead. "Shot in the back by a yellow-bellied so-and-so by the name of McCall," he said. "He should have listened to me."

Dr. Carver went on and entered dental school in California but he didn't stay long—just long enough to earn himself the "Doctor" tag which stayed with him the rest of his life. The tooth-pulling business lost its hold on him the day he went to a gun club and blasted all the targets in sight. He was such a good shot that word got around and one of the leading newspapers carried a story about him. The next thing he knew, some enterprising men had put up the money to launch him on a career that was to take him all over the globe and earn him the title of "Champion Rifleshot of the World."

By special request he exhibited at Sandringham, England, on April 13,1879, before the Queen, the Prince and Princess of Wales, the Duke and Duchess of Connaught, and members of the royal household. Two days later he received a complimentary letter from the Prince of Wales, who was to become Edward the VII of England. The letter was accompanied by a gold pin set with diamonds known as the Prince of Wales Feathers, and he was the only American ever to receive it. Later on that same trip, thirty thousand soldiers cheered him when he exhibited his marksmanship before Sir Robert Peel of Aldershot

In Germany some weeks later, Emperor Wilhelm I of Germany titled him *der Shutzen Konig* (King of Marksmen) at an exhibition before an audience that included Bismarck, Baron von Moltke and his staff, and the Grand

Duke Albert of Austria. During the course of this exhibition the Emperor pulled a crown piece from his pocket and told Dr. Carver that if he shot a hole through the coin while it was in the air he would be satisfied that there was no trickery involved in his amazing marksmanship.

"With your permission," said Dr. Carver, "I will not only shoot a hole through it but I will put a bullet through Your Majesty's head on the raised surface of the coin." When he had made good his boast, Baron von Moltke threw his arms around him and said, "Oh for an army of such as you!" Later the Kaiser sent Dr. Carver a magnificent diamond ring, and when he came back to the United States two years later he had a chest full of jewels and medals and more glory than he could believe. He was quoted as saying that the only reason he came back then was because he got homesick for a piece of custard pie.

Not long afterward he ran into his old friend Buffalo Bill, and the two of them hit on the idea of putting together a company for the purpose of presenting melodramas about the old West. It was called "The Wild West-Cody and Carver's Rocky Mountain and Prairie Exhibition," and they opened in Omaha in 1883. It was highly successful, but unfortunately the partnership didn't last. Both men were so hot-tempered that the enterprise finally blew up in a quarrel that left them bitter enemies for life.

The following spring there were two Wild West shows in the country —"Cody's Show" and "Carver's Show"—and the rivalry between them was intense. They fought each other from one end of the country to the other, a favorite trick being to find out where the other had a show opening and get there first to skim off the town's money.

In the end Buffalo Bill's show lasted longer, but Dr. Carver had his innings, for in 1885 he attracted world-wide attention by undertaking a shooting exhibition that called for endurance as well as skill. He set out to achieve a record of ten thousand hits a day for six days running. He shot at what were called "glass balls," balls made of resin, which shattered like glass when struck with a bullet. Sometimes in order to get in his ten thousand hits a day he would shoot on into the night by the light of flares. People everywhere were astonished by his supreme marksmanship as well as his amazing physical endurance. The guns became so hot from such rapid shooting that he had a barrel of water sitting nearby and an attendant whose job it was to dunk the guns to cool them off.

Before he gave up the Wild West show business entirely Dr. Carver decided to take his troupe to Europe. He said the real reason he went was that he heard Buffalo Bill was going and he had to go in order to spite him. After Europe he went to Australia for apparently the same reason, and it was while he was on this trip that he was launched on still another career.

The playwrights, after hearing him talk about his life on the plains, decided to write a play about him. They called it *The Trapper* and got Dr. Carver to play the lead. Later they wrote one called *The Scout,* which was even more successful and in which he also played the lead. He brought this play back to San Francisco and was soon thrilling American audiences with it from coast to coast.

It was like nothing anyone had ever seen before on a stage. It required a cast of hundreds—cowboys, pioneers, Indians, and a herd of horses which were brought onto the stage in wild action scenes. It was while he was appearing in *The Scout* that he first happened on the idea of teaching horses to dive.

In the play there was a scene in which Dr. Carver rode a horse over a bridge. It was rigged so that when a stage hand pulled a lever the bridge fell out from under him. He always reached up and caught hold of an upright and hung on, while the horse plunged on down into a river of water which flowed through the middle of the stage. It didn't hurt the horse, but it scared him so that he balked at crossing the bridge a second time. As a consequence Dr. Carver had to use a different horse every night.

This worked out all right until the night they ran out of horses. Dr. Carver suggested that they try an old faithful of his, Silver King. King had been across the bridge before, but Dr. Carver thought he might be willing to try it again, and he was. In fact, after the bridge had dropped out from under him and dumped him in the water, King trotted back up the embankment, ready for an encore. It was then that Dr. Carver hit on the idea of teaching horses to dive for entertainment purposes.

When the play finally closed he began training high-diving horses in earnest, and it was from this beginning that his present act had risen. It had been in existence ten years by the time I saw it, and thousands of people all over the United States had applauded "Carver's High-Diving Horse Act and the Girl-in-Red."

The write-up ended with the announcement that the fair was closing tomorrow night and that anybody who hadn't seen the act should, because it was a spectacle not to be missed.

When I had finished reading I put the paper down. All I could hope was that Dr. Carver hadn't already hired a girl to do the riding, because I knew beyond a shadow of a doubt that I was that girl.

Two

The next morning I got up early and dragged Jac out of bed. It was Sunday and I didn't have to go to work and she didn't have to go to school. "Come on," I said. "We've got to hurry." She didn't need to ask where. She put on a sailor dress and I a blue serge skirt and white blouse, and we hurried out without breakfast.

When we reached the hotel it was only nine o'clock, but the desk clerk told us Dr. Carver wasn't there. For a moment I experienced a sinking sensation, thinking he had already checked out, but the clerk added, "I think he's gone down to see the submarine."

The submarine the clerk had referred to had been the object of everyone's attention since its arrival. Hopefully Jac and I began to walk through the park leading down to the river and hadn't gone far when we saw a tall, erect figure coming toward us.

With Dr. Carver were his son and daughter and the rider named Vivian, all of whom I had met the evening Mother had dragged me to the hotel lobby. As they approached, I saw signs of recognition on their faces.

I cannot recall after all these years our exact conversation, but I apparently said that I had seen the act the night before and had changed my mind about riding. What happened next remains hazy. The conversation shifted and changed, and then they were saying good-by and walking away.

"What did I do?" I asked Jac, dumbfounded.

"You didn't do anything," she said.

"Well, why didn't they say anything about my joining the act then?"

"I don't know," she said, then added, "maybe they don't want you."

That much seemed fairly obvious. "But," I puzzled, "if they didn't they could have told me so."

"Yeah," Jac agreed.

I was confounded and remained so. There seemed no reason to it. Then one day about three months later I came home to find a letter. It was from Dr. Carver, who wrote, "If you still want to learn to ride the diving horses, reply at this address."

I sat down and answered right away. Of course I expected to hear from him immediately, but one week passed, then two, then three, and still no word came. Just as dust was beginning to settle over my newly revived hopes, Dr. Carver himself appeared at my boardinghouse while I was at work, but told my landlady that he would be back to talk to me. I waited that evening in vain. He didn't come until the next afternoon. Mother happened to be with me, so he invited us both to dinner to talk about the job.

During the meal he said he was glad to find that I still wanted to ride the diving horses. He made no explanation for not having taken me up on my job acceptance back in October and I refrained from asking for any. The point was, I was getting another chance to ride and I wasn't looking a gift horse in the mouth. When he asked how soon I could leave, I said the next day. This pleased him, because he was anxious to get back to Florida, where the rest of the troupe was in winter quarters.

I had already mentally packed everything I owned and was in the process of imagining myself waving good-by from the train, when suddenly Mother piped up. "Sonora," she said, "are you sure this is what you want to do?" There was no mistaking the worry in her face and voice.

"Why, of course I'm sure!" I retorted. "What do you mean, 'am I sure? You sound as if you don't want me to go."

"It isn't that I don't want you to go," she said. "It's just that I'm afraid you'll get hurt."

"You weren't afraid last fall. Why are you afraid now?"

"Well, last fall you weren't really going," she explained. "It was just something to talk about. Now—well, now it's different."

I should have been prepared for such a shift, but I was not. She had been so completely sold on my going that I never anticipated a reversal. I don't know what I would have done had it not been for Dr. Carver. He saw what a quandary I was in, took over, and soon placated Mother. He was, I was to find in the course of our acquaintanceship, a master placater.

Half afraid something would happen to change someone's mind before I got away, I hurried back to the boardinghouse and packed all my things. Then I went out to the cottage to spend the night and say good-by to my sisters and brothers.

Perhaps those last few hours at home should have been filled with nostalgia; but, to be truthful, I was so excited about going that there wasn't room for any backward glances. Fortunately the children were equally excited, so there were no tears.

It was different, however, the next day at the station. Suddenly I realized I was leaving and that, no matter what happened, things would never again be the same. There seemed to be two parts of myself then—a part that loved my family and would miss them, and a part that was wild to go.

Now they all stood on the platform, waving good-by to me, and as the train pulled away and the track spooled out behind me I knew that I was starting a new life.

Three

I think it is important for me to give my impressions of Dr. Carver, for although I was excited at the prospect of learning to ride and dive on the horses, it is doubtful that I would have joined the act had I not realized from the first what an unusual person he was. It was more than his press clippings. It was the man himself.

I have described him as tall and commanding and going on eighty-four. I have not said that he had a big strong face and big strong hands, which, though stiff and old, were nevertheless extremely impressive. He also had the air of an impresario, which he had acquired during his years in show business. Total strangers noticed it and behaved accordingly; it would have gone against some law of nature had they behaved otherwise.

He was a descendant of one of the first governors of Massachusetts and a long line of doctors and lawyers and professors. His father had been a doctor, and in the years of Dr. Carver's growing up he had been fairly well-to-do. For some reason I never understood, Dr. Carver and his father did not get along. In fact, his father treated him so cruelly that he ran away from home when he was only eleven years old.

I suppose a runaway child was not so rare in those days, but it is unlikely that many of them succeeded to the extent that Dr. Carver did. It is also unlikely for him to have emerged with such presence had he not inherited a sense of dignity. I am a great believer in heredity, and it pleased me to learn many years later that the family motto engraved on a gold-headed cane belonging to Governor Carver was "Blood Will Tell."

I hope I haven't made him sound like a stuffed shirt, because that he was not. He was aloof and standoffish with people of his own station, but with his inferiors he showed a warmth that endeared him to them immediately. I can best describe his attitude toward them as one of friendly awareness, and as a result they went out of their way to help him. Yet he still managed it so that under no circumstances did they treat him with familiarity. This is a difficult balance to achieve, but he achieved it and held to it throughout the time I knew him.

Of course by the time I came along he had passed his zenith in so far as his physical prowess was concerned. The glittering brilliance of being the champion rifleshot of the world was gone. He was likely to be crotchety at times, lacking in patience and resilience, covetous of his own comfort, but he was, on the other hand, neither a braggart nor bombastic, both of which he might have been under the circumstances. He loved to talk about his past and did often, but he always told his stories in such a delightful manner that there was never any resentment on the part of the listener.

All, or almost all, of his characteristics were obvious to me from the first, but I was so much in awe of him on the trip to Florida that I hardly spoke. That was not necessary, however, for his love for storytelling took over, and before we reached our destination I had digested a great deal about his son and daughter, the act and its history.

Allen (called Al by everyone) helped his father train and take care of the horses; his daughter Lorena was a rider and had been riding since her early teens. She had injured a leg muscle the year before, however. This accident had required some surgery, so she hadn't been able to ride during the current season. When spring came they hoped the doctors would release her so that she could go out on a separate circuit with Al. They tried to keep two versions of the diving act working at the same time in different places in order to double the income from it.

I did not know the actual amount of money the act earned per contract until many years later, although I knew it must be considerable. All I knew was that I would be receiving fifty dollars a week, which in 1924 was a great deal of money. As a bookkeeper in Savannah's largest department store, I had been earning only fifteen dollars a week, and this was considered about standard pay. By taking a job with the act I had more than tripled my income, and later in the season the pay would go even higher when I began riding as many as five times a day—up to $125 a week! During the winter when the act was not working my salary would stop, but even then I would receive a traveling allowance, my board and room, and whatever medical expenses I might have. All in all, it was more money than I had ever encountered in my life.

The idea of so much money made me a little giddy, but I knew even then, young as I was, that money wasn't everything. To me it wasn't important at all unless it included an equal amount of experience. Ever since early childhood I had had a craving for life, and as I grew older it had not diminished. I had once shocked a friend by telling her I'd be disappointed if I ever made an ocean voyage and didn't get seasick.

"Get seasick!" she had said. "Nobody wants to get seasick!"

I said I did. I said I wanted to get seasick and throw up and have to hang onto the rail. How else was I ever going to know what being seasick was like?

Outside of the bits of information I gleaned from Dr. Carver on the four-hour trip to Florida, there is little to recall except one episode I shall never forget.

We had gone to the dining car in the evening and then headed back to our seats. On the way I stopped by the ladies' room to wash my hands and while doing so had taken off my rings. Sometime later I remembered I had left the rings lying on a little shelf above the basin. My first thought, naturally, was to rush back to the washroom.

The difficulty was that Dr. Carver had now settled back for a nap, and his enormous frame was stretched out so that his legs were blocking the aisle. There was nothing for me to do but jump over him since I didn't want to wake him, and jumping is what I tried to do. I was almost into the aisle when I heard a whoop, an awful roar. It came from Dr. Carver and was as terrifying as anything I had ever heard in my life. I could see out of the corner of my eye that he was grabbing at his hip and knew instinctively he was reaching for a gun. Then I was out and down the aisle, sprinting for the washroom.

I found my rings where I had left them and then went back to my seat. There I found him sitting with his arms crossed, looking stormy and black.

"Don't ever do that again," he said. "Don't ever touch me while I'm sleeping."

"I won't," I said. "I'm sorry. I had to—"

"Never mind," he said. "When you move, move like a lady, not like a damn grasshopper."

"No, sir," I said, "I won't."

Later he told me that the whoop was left over from his days on the plains, when a whoop in time meant the difference between having a scalp and not having one. If a man did not wake shouting and reaching for a gun, his pelt was likely to wave from a tepee.

By the time I joined the troupe in Jacksonville, they had been there almost four months. Most of what is known as "winter quarters" had therefore already passed.

Winter quarters is a kind of hibernation period that occurs every year. The fairs and amusement parks all over the country close down during the cold months, so that people in show business are forced to retire. The time, however, is not wasted. During these months they do all the things they haven't had time to do before. They mend equipment, devise new acts, and make their next season's engagements, so that when spring comes their itineraries are fixed and they know where they are going.

Show people have a reputation as brawlers second only, I think, to longshoremen. In some cases I'm sure it's deserved, but for the most part it is as exaggerated as most other stories about them. After all, self-discipline is more important for them than for other people because usually their lives depend on fitness in a way that the ordinary person's does not. All an aerial artist needs is a second off his timing to find himself lying on the sawdust, and timing comes not only from practice but from constant fitness as well.

Of course loss of life does not always result from loose living, but loss of skill does; and when that goes, so does the professional position that has been built with such painstaking care. Nobody stays at the top very long unless he is dedicated and willing to make sacrifices.

Hence show people work constantly on fitness during these winter months, keeping muscles firm and taut by daily practice. If their act depends on animals rather than themselves, as is often the case, then they work at keeping the animals fit.

Most animals need to be kept in training as much for discipline as for anything else. Lion and tiger acts would go to pieces if the discipline were relaxed for very long. For the Carver horses, however, this was not the case. Once a horse had been trained to go off the tower, he never seemed to forget how to do it nor to lose his skill or style. As a performer, he could be counted on to maintain almost status quo. This relieved Al and Dr. Carver from having to rehearse constantly and they had only to be certain that the horses were properly stabled and fed.

While in winter quarters the diving horses had extra-roomy stalls with foot-deep pine shavings spread on the ground. This was to provide them with bedding which some people apparently were not aware they needed. During my years with the act I heard people say, "Why, look! They're lying down!" This always made Dr. Carver very angry; he said all horses would lie down to rest if they were given decent bedding. When the pine shavings became soiled they were taken out and replaced with fresh ones.

Each horse had his own bucket of water, which hung from a nail in his stall. It had his name printed on it in white and it was always kept filled with fresh water. This was another of Dr. Carver's dicta. He said horses should be able to drink when they were thirsty, not when somebody else decided they were.

Twice a day in the winter they were fed barley, Texas prairie hay, or oats and were also let out to graze. During the summer, when they were working, they were fed three times—morning, late afternoon, and at night after a performance, when the diver was given two quarts of oats and the non-divers one. Their hay was always put down on the ground and dampened a little in order to settle the dust. Putting it on the ground rather than in a manger also gave them a chance to stamp it in order to get the chaff out and keep it from being sucked up into their lungs. This was the way a horse did it when left to himself on the range, and Dr. Carver tried to let them hold to their natural habits as much as possible.

Baskets of carrots and apples were always kept around for treats, and sugar was given each performer after he made his dive. The only other time they got sugar was at Christmas. Of course the horses all loved sugar but had to be taught to eat it, since it was foreign to their natural diet. A lump was moistened and crushed in the hand and then smeared on their lips. They licked it off and, once they had learned the taste, they would take it in lump form from a person's hand.

They were constantly curried and combed and carefully dried after diving. One of the first things I learned about a horse named Klatawah was to stay away from him when he was being dried. I was standing in his stall one day when the groom was drying him, and Klatawah was giving the groom a time. He was especially ticklish in his underquarters and was dancing around, so that the groom could not get at him. Thinking I'd be helpful, I got an apple and offered it to the horse. He took not only the apple but also my hand and arm! It frightened me half to death, but the next moment he released me, completely unbitten. Nevertheless, after that I stayed away from him when he was being dried.

Al always clipped their coats in the spring so they would come out new and glossy, but he never roached their manes because they all had beautiful ones, except Klatawah, who as a thoroughbred had inherited a stringy one. His was trimmed to stand up stiff and starchy, making him look much younger than he was.

Dr. Carver had told me that from time to time they got in trouble with the Society for the Prevention of Cruelty to Animals, whose sometimes overzealous members decided the horses were being mistreated. At such times the SPCA would send a veterinarian to examine them. Each time the vet gave them a clean bill of health. The usual conclusion was that he had never seen healthier, more beautifully kept animals in his We. Once, however, in California, a group issued an order restraining the Carvers from presenting the act until it could be investigated. This made Al so mad that he put one of the horses on a truck with a sign on it that read, "I'm being taken to jail for jumping in a tank of water," and proceeded to drive all around town.

On the day of the hearing he took the horse down to the courthouse and staked her out on the lawn. He wanted to take her inside the courthouse for the judge to see but decided he'd better not when he found that the steps were marble. Since diving horses were never shod (to keep them from slipping when they were diving), it was safer to leave Lightning on the lawn. Al did, however, tell the judge he had her outside and that he'd appreciate it if the judge would come see for himself. The judge recessed court, went out and looked at the horse, and when he got back in threw the whole case out of court.

I arrived in Jacksonville to find the horses stabled at what had once been a race track. One line of paddocks was fixed up for the horses so that each horse had a separate stall. The first morning Dr. Carver took me on a tour. I could see names on the doors as we approached the paddock, but there was no sign of the horses until Dr. Carver cupped his hand to his mouth and shouted, "Where are Daddy's horses?"

Instantly five heads shot out of five openings: a gray head, a white head, two with roan markings, and at the end of the row a sorrel who tossed his head and whinnied. They were all so beautiful, I sucked in my breath.

Dr. Carver went first to the sorrel, whose door bore the name "Klatawah," and took the big head in his big hands and pulled it down to his own. He held it there for a moment, petting the horse's hard jaw, and as I watched I knew with a lump in my throat that there was a great deal of affection between them. Then I gravitated toward the only one I felt I "knew"—the Duchess of Lightning, who had performed the night at the fair. When I put my hand up to pet her she didn't back away. She looked at me a moment and then whickered slightly, as if she were speaking.

After a few minutes Dr. Carver came to where I was standing and took me up the line, stopping to say something appropriate to each one and telling me something about him. That done, he led me over to the barn where Al was working.

As we walked away I looked back at the heads of the five brave horses which, in the years to come, were to be such vital and dearly loved parts of my life.

Four

We left Jacksonville about three weeks later and arrived in Durham on the first of April. Since we were not due to open at Lakeside Amusement Park until May 20, this gave me almost seven weeks to get in shape.

This was not as simple as it would once have been, for I had gained fifteen pounds since I'd seen the Carvers in October. Adler's Department Store, where I worked, sold delicious tuna fish sandwiches and coffee with whipped cream and superb lemon pie. The results had been calamitous, and I now weighed 140 pounds.

The fact that the gain was noticeable was brought immediately to my attention. Al had no sooner met us at the station in Jacksonville than he made some remark about their horses not being accustomed to carrying over 135 pounds. "And," he had added, cutting his eyes at me, "we like them to carry less."

I came to understand why. It is difficult for a horse to pull out at the incline at the front of the tank if a rider is too heavy. Also, it is easier for a lightweight person to move quickly. This is very important, since moving quickly will help the horse to make a good dive out of a bad dive. Finally, and strictly from a show-business standpoint, a small rider on a big horse has a more dramatic effect on an audience than a big rider on a big horse.

Unfortunately there was little I could do about losing weight but to cut down on my eating. Dr. Carver didn't believe in dieting, however, so I took walks and swam in the tank, neither of which helped much. My condition demanded something in the nature of a crash program, which, although I didn't know it, I was about to get.

Al had stayed behind with the horses in Florida until we could see what accommodations there were for them in Durham. Having found them to be adequate, Dr. Carver wired him to come on, and the day after Al's arrival was the signal for my training to begin.

Since the diving horses were never used as saddle horses they had to be exercised artificially. Each one was put on a long rope held by one of the grooms or Al or Dr. Carver and circled at a gallop around him. Being healthy animals, they reared and kicked like colts. On that never-to-be-forgotten morning, Dr. Carver gave me some old khaki army riding pants to put on over my bathing suit and some sneakers for my feet. The unbecoming pants, which laced up on the inside of the legs, were to protect my legs from the abrasive effects of the pounding until the muscles of my legs and thighs developed enough to enable me to hold myself in place. When I had them on I was boosted up on the back of Klatawah and firmly commanded to "Stick!"

Sticking was, I found, most difficult. I had no saddle, no bridle, no stirrups to brace myself, and the horse had no bit in his teeth. In short, there was nothing with which to guide him or for me to hold onto except the strap of the diving harness, which consisted of two leather bands, one fitted around the base of the horse's neck and the other around his body, both held in place by connecting straps and a martingale.

To add to my troubles, Klatawah, although the oldest horse of the five, was also the liveliest. Who would have thought that a horse the equivalent of a seventy-year-old man could have galloped the way he did! I slipped and slid all over his back from one side to the other, finally dangling dangerously off to one side at a flying angle. When he felt me slide off he immediately came to a halt and waited patiently while the groom cupped his hand for me to put my foot in and boosted me up again. Then he continued his dashing around and around until I was battered and dizzy.

It was hot and dirty on the lot, and the dust that fogged the air was soon sticking all over me, my own perspiration acting as a base. I could not have been more grateful when the groom finally slowed Klatawah to a walk and allowed me to slide off.

My knees were quivering as I limped away, but I hadn't gone far when I heard Dr. Carver say, "Where are you going, Sonora?"

"To get dressed," I replied, wondering how I had managed to avoid shattering my vocal cords.

"No, you're not," he said. "You've got three more horses to exercise."

In my state of semi-collapse I found this hard to believe, but Dr. Carver was the boss and I would not have dreamed of arguing. So I clambered on the second horse and, after him, the third. By the time they ran the fourth one out I was near collapse, but I threw myself on her and somehow managed to stay there. I was so tired when I finished, however, that I let my head drop forward as I slid off her back, which proved to be a mistake, for just at that moment she threw her head back and it crashed into my nose. Instantly blood shot from both nostrils as if someone had turned on a faucet.

It hurt terribly and by itself would have been enough to flatten me, but taken in combination with my bedraggled state it proved almost lethal. I swayed for a moment, wondering if I would drop, and then I heard Dr. Carver say, "That was your fault."

For a moment I wondered if I had heard him right. It seemed such a heartless thing to say under the circumstances. Then I realized he had. "*My* fault!" I blazed with the last ounce of my strength.

"Yes," he said, "it was. You were careless and let your head drop down. Next time she's liable to knock out your teeth."

It was brutal of him to chastise me at such a time, but I was to find that this was his way. He seemed to have a theory that sympathy bolstered weakness and that strength was begotten by strength. Anyway, I was the momentary victim of whatever he thought and, though I felt like crying, I didn't. In place of tears I turned on my heel and strode away to my dressing room, telling myself he was a tyrant and a bully and that I'd die rather than cry in front of him and give him that satisfaction.

After a couple of days of ground training I was black and blue all over and so sore when night came I could hardly move. I couldn't touch myself without whimpering or move without a moan. All my muscles felt as if they'd been tied in granny knots and the tissues as if they'd been boiled. Still I knew, or at least hoped, that soon that part would be over and I'd be whole again.

During the time of my misery the platform was being built and day by day rose higher, like a dinosaur skeleton. The ridged spine was a series of sills (two-by-fours) put up in the ground at four-foot intervals. They were staggered in height so that those at the foot of the ramp were very low and those at the top forty feet high. After the men had them in place they laid uprights on the ground and then pulled them up against the sills with ropes. These were then nailed into place in a pattern of ribbon and crossbraces in order to give the tower strength. After the skeleton was up, flooring was laid on the ramp and a handrail was put up on either side.

At the top, the ramp was joined to the main part of the tower by means of a six-foot aisle which leveled off from the ramp and slanted slightly down at the point of drop-off. Here a series of planks was nailed against the uprights to form one wide piece. This was called the kickoff board because it gave the horse something to kick against when he took off. It was padded so that he couldn't slip. The sides of the platform were padded, too, to help protect the rider from friction burns that often resulted when a horse dived off at an angle rather than straight ahead and threw or scraped the rider against one of the uprights.

After the tower was completed the tank was dug, and it was enormous—forty feet long, twenty feet wide, and eleven feet deep. Both Al and Dr. Carver watched carefully the entire time it was being dug to make sure that all the measurements were correct.

The depth was particularly important and had been arrived at only after several years of trial and error. They had first experimented with one sixteen feet deep but found that the horse was so buoyant that at such a depth he didn't go down far enough in the water for his feet to touch the bottom. Touching bottom was important, for it gave the horse the control he otherwise lacked. If he didn't touch he was liable to come up tail to the audience, sideways, rolling, or what have you. At the head of the tank an incline was placed which the horse used to pull himself out of the tank.

To keep the pool from leaking or draining, it was lined with an enormous canvas attached around the sides by large grommets that were put over stakes driven into the ground. When the tank was filled it held thirty-five thousand gallons of water and made an excellent swimming pool for exercising between performances.

When the whole structure was finished the tower and ramp were painted white and lights were strung along the railing. Streamers of lights were also run from the top of the platform to the ground. These had to be carefully placed so that none were reflected in the pool. To a horse a reflection is not a reflection but the real thing and, being a sensible animal, he is not going to dive into a string of lights. There was also the matter of spotlights which were thrown on the performers after they got up to the top. These, too, had to be placed with extreme care, for light shining in the horse's eyes could blind or confuse him. Therefore, the spots were aimed to shine from either above or behind.

All in all, it was expensive, a single tower costing something in the neighborhood of a thousand dollars. This was, however, always at the expense of the park or fair, a part of the Carver contract.

The process of building was exciting to me and I watched the tower go up plank by plank. For some reason I could not fathom, my constant attendance at the project seemed to annoy Dr. Carver, and one day he asked me why I stayed around so close. I told him I wanted to learn how it was done and he said I didn't need to know, which was an answer he might have given anyone but which didn't set too well with me.

He did not, however, forbid my climbing it once it was finished. When I did, the first look down from that height caused me to step back involuntarily and grasp the railing on either side. Still grasping the railing, I bent forward and peered cautiously over the edge again to see if I had been mistaken, but no, it still seemed much higher from there looking down than it had appeared on the ground looking up. By the time I had climbed the tower a few more times the distance no longer bothered me and I was able to gaze down or out or wherever I chose without the slightest feeling of uneasiness.

When the tower was up and the tank dug and filled, the workmen began to build another platform, much lower, within the tower uprights. This one was only twelve feet from the water and was used for training purposes, both for new riders and new horses. This height was sufficient to give the horse the feel of the jump without frightening him to death, and the same was true for the rider.

Before I began my training from this low tower, however, Dr. Carver decided he wanted me to learn to do some dives. These were not ordinary dives, which I already knew, but trick dives and swimming stunts that I would be able to use in a special act at parks and fairs if so requested. Lorena had added some dives to her riding act, and the crowds had responded well. Having decided I should do the same, Dr. Carver ordered a fireman's ladder and had a portable pedestal built. With the ladder and the pedestal he could then promote me to any height on the tower he chose and not only teach me fancy dives but gradually accustom me to perform from the forty-foot height.

I was eager to learn dives and swimming tricks, but Dr. Carver nearly removed all my enthusiasm. Sitting in the shade in a comfortable chair, he would give me orders. "All right, three somersaults backward, a log roll, and finish up with the water wheel."

This took a little doing, but I would no sooner accomplish that mixture than he would say, "All right, now a swan dive, followed by the dead man's float, and after that the waltzing trick."

I'd clamber up the ladder, panting and beginning to change color, but no matter how advanced the state of my exhaustion, if I so much as stopped for a moment to get my breath he would glower at me and say, "If you're too tired to practice you might as well get dressed."

Finally one day when I was fed to the teeth I snapped, "Don't hurry me! It makes me nervous."

For a minute it stopped Dr. Carver cold. I had never talked back to him before. Nobody did. Al and Lorena let him run the show in his own way (no matter how much better they thought they might have run it) and never gave advice except in a roundabout manner, tactfully indicating that the suggestion originally had been his.

Now he looked at me from beneath the brim of his hat, which, I had learned, was not a hat but a weather vane. If it was on straight, things were going well; at an angle, he was feeling cocky. If it was on the back of his head, he had things to settle and you'd better watch out. Today it was on at an angle. Suddenly he laughed. "Makes you nervous, does it?" he said. "Well, now that's a pity. You go get your dress on and I'll buy you a lemonade." He was apparently as unpredictable as the weather itself.

By this time about three weeks had passed in Durham and I had already lost weight. I had also developed some new muscles and no longer ached all over. I knew I was ready to dive, and Dr. Carver confirmed this a few days later by telling Al he was to take me up on the low tower and show me how to stand.

Standing was necessary when mounting the horse from the low tower because there wasn't enough room for the rider to sit on the rail. After the horse came up and got into position all the space was filled because the area within the low tower was cramped. Al placed me on the left-hand side of the railing and then stood across from me on the opposite side.

Dr. Carver went to get the horse ready. I put on my helmet and listened while Al gave me some instructions.

"When the horse drops his feet forward onto the kickoff board, pull back with your weight; not on the harness, but with your body, so as to help keep your balance. A rider is able to think during the action of the dive only after some experience. In the beginning the brain merely registers impressions, and one of the most vivid is false. When the horse first drops his feet over the edge, you'll have the feeling that he's going to turn a somersault and that you're going off over his head, but you won't, and once he actually dives, this sensation will leave. In the meantime don't panic. One girl we were training got so scared she let go of the harness the same time the horse kicked off, and she shot off his back like a cannon. She landed in the front of the tank, and all that saved her from breaking her neck was that she landed flat."

With this amusing little story to cheer me I waited for the horse. When Dr. Carver was ready, Al signaled that we were, and Klatawah started up the ramp. The sound of his hoofs was dull thunder as 1250 pounds of sorrel-colored energy hurtled toward me. I suddenly had the feeling that we were the only living creatures in the otherwise silent and motionless world. Then he was beside me and Al reached out and stopped him.

Klatawah was the liveliest of all the horses, and being halted made him impatient I was no sooner on his back than he dropped his feet over the side and dived. For a split second there was an open space between us and the water, and then we hit it smoothly. I heard the water gurgling and bubbling around us as we went down, down, down, and then I felt his feet touch bottom and he gave a strong push upward. Almost at once we surfaced and I was still on him. When he pulled out at the incline a few moments later, I slipped off his back and was as proud as if I'd just brought in a winner at the Kentucky Derby.

I had imagined that Dr. Carver would be equally proud of me, but he wasn't even there. Al sensed my disappointment and said, "Never mind. He doesn't watch the dives after a performer is trained. Don't worry. I'll tell you whether you're doing anything wrong. Come on, let's try it again."

As I rounded the ramp to the back to make my second ride, there was Dr. Carver. He gave me a little half smile and I knew what it meant. "That was all right," it seemed to say, "but don't get swell-headed about it."

This time Al told me how to improve my ride. "You ducked your head a little too soon. Wait until the horse is in mid-air. And when he dives, sit tighter. The closer you sit him, the better. When he comes up from the bottom and starts swimming, let go of the harness and get hold of his mane. This gives him more freedom of movement and makes the swimming easier for him. And remember that when his feet touch bottom he'll throw his head back, so be careful to keep *your* head to one side or you'll get your nose broken."

As Al coached me, the odds between me and the hospital seemed to get smaller, but it turned out that I rode Klatawah a second time and a third time, and each time I came out unwounded. In fact, I rode him twice a day for the next three weeks, and by the middle of May I had made twenty-one dives from the low tower.

The morning after my twenty-first jump, as I walked away to my dressing room, Dr. Carver announced without any preamble, "You're ready for the top."

My face burst into a big smile. I had been waiting for this! Then, as if afraid he might say something congratulatory, he turned around and walked off.

Still, his grouchiness could not dampen my spirits. I was delighted with myself and waited for the following morning with an almost childish impatience. When it came finally I got up and shot out of the park and put on my suit.

Until then I had had to wear the army riding pants over my suit, but now I was able to shed them. There would no longer be the danger of a friction burn, at least not as much as there had been within the narrow confines of the low tower, so for the first time I wore the trade-mark of my act— a modest red wool bathing suit with a rounded neck and a long torso.

I put on heavy socks to protect my ankles and over them canvas swimming shoes. I also had my helmet, which was a "must." Dr. Carver insisted his riders wear one in order to prevent serious injury should they get kicked by a horse. This could happen if a rider fell off in the tank and got caught beneath murderously thrashing hoofs.

I looked around for the groom, who should have had Klatawah harnessed, but neither horse nor groom was in sight. Searching further, I walked around to the barn, where I found Al and Dr. Carver deep in conversation. Al was sorting brushes and scrapers, and as I walked up I caught the last of Dr. Carver's words, ". . . get a new rider."

For a moment I was jolted, thinking he meant someone to replace me; then I realized that he meant someone to replace Lorena. She had gone to see her doctor in New Orleans shortly after we arrived in Durham and had written her father the week before, saying that the doctor didn't want her to ride for another year.

They continued their discussion even though I stood close by, and neither of them acknowledged my presence by so much as a lifted eyebrow. I stood first on one foot and then the other and finally blurted out, "When are you going to harness my horse so I can ride from the high tower?"

Dr. Carver looked at me as if I had just dropped off the moon. "When you make your first ride from the tower," he said, "it will be for the benefit of an audience."

It was my turn to be astonished. "But that's seven days away!" I said. "The park doesn't open until the twentieth. I'll forget everything I've learned!"

"No, you won't," answered Al. "It's like riding a bicycle or swimming. It's not something you forget. Believe me. I know." But for all his sympathetic words, his face had taken on the same lines as his father's. I could see he was equally implacable.

For a moment I stood looking from one to the other and then turned and walked away. There was obviously nothing I could do.

I spent the next week roaming the lot all by myself and silently hating everyone. I brooded over Dr. Carver's thoughtlessness and told myself he had no right. Not that I was afraid I'd be hurt; I was afraid I'd look like a fool. I didn't care what I maimed or broke, just so I looked as if I knew what I was doing. And how could I, if I'd never done it before?

This was a bad time for me, made worse by the fact that Al left two days before we opened. He had to see to the setting up of a platform and tank in Texas, where he would do his first show. With him gone and Lorena still in New Orleans, I was left alone with Dr. Carver. Communication between us, which had been sputtering on and off for so long, seemed to have become permanently short-circuited. The result was a series of minor skirmishes in which I always seemed to be the loser.

I asked him one day what I should do about the audience after I made my ride.

"After you dismount, face the audience and make a nice bow."

"Bow!" I said. "I'd feel like a fool!"

"Then do anything you damn please," he snapped.

Our relationship was indeed wearing thin, but I didn't know how thin until I went out to the park the day we were to open and found Dr. Carver pacing. He had already accused me a number of times of being unduly nervous and had suggested that I calm down. Now he was kicking up more dust than I had ever kicked and it made me angry. All that week I had been bashing the jitters over the head and getting lectured about it, and here he was at the last minute coming down with his own case of the jitters. So far I had consoled myself with the thought that he wouldn't let me do it if he didn't think I could, but here he was, blasting my only prop right out from under me.

Later I learned he was always nervous on the opening day of any engagement, but I didn't know it then, so it was no help to me. All I could do was hold onto the few nerves I had left and count away the hours.

Mr. Foster, the manager of the park, had advertised our act as the featured free act of the grandstand opening, and as a consequence, long before appearance time, thousands of people were standing around the rope that separated the tank from the crowd. From my dressing room I could hear their voices, and as they grew louder my own excitement increased. I had to fight to keep myself calm enough to get dressed, but at last I had the suit on and the socks and shoes. Finally, and with extreme reluctance, I put on the bathrobe.

Had it been my bathrobe or almost anyone else's it wouldn't have been so bad, but the bathrobe was Dr. Carver's and it wrapped around me twice. I had begged for a fringed shawl to wear as I walked to and from the tower, but he had barked an immediate and pre-emptive "No!" He was terribly conservative, severely disapproving of anything that smacked of "flappers," and felt completely justified in handing me his bathrobe.

To appreciate the situation fully, one need only recall that he stood six feet four and weighed more than two hundred pounds, whereas I stood five feet six and weighed 125. The bathrobe, moreover, a gray wool affair, when bunched and tied around me resembled nothing so much as the hide of an old bull elephant. I had to keep hitching it up to avoid stepping on it and I could not have felt more unglamorous if I'd had the ears and trunk too.

As we walked toward the tower we had to force our way. People stood hundreds deep in places. When we finally got to the ramp I saw that George, our groom, had made it somehow and was standing there with Klatawah. I took off the robe and laid it over the railing and began to climb.

I don't remember what thoughts went through my mind or even whether I had any thoughts, because a kind of numbness took over and I moved like a robot. All I remember is that when I got to the top I discovered I was no longer nervous and unsure. I looked down at seven thousand faces turned up to me, and their expressions of excitement and anticipation made me feel humble as well as proud. I wanted to do my best for them and somehow knew I would.

I waved to the crowd, boosted myself up on the railing, and put on my helmet. When I signaled George to send Klatawah up, he began to turn him to build up the horse's momentum, then sent him into the runway. Klatawah's hoofs hit the ramp with a crash.

The whole tower vibrated and shook as he rushed up at me, and I knew that in a split second he would be going past. Then he was there and I grabbed for the harness and swung myself into place. As he drew up at the head of the platform I was aware I had mounted him right. But the real test was ahead of me. I had to stay on him, come up from the water on him, and ride him out of the tank. If I failed to do any of these things I would have failed as a rider—and I wanted to be a good rider more than anything else.

I was anxious to be off and get it over with, but Klatawah was not. He was a fast enough diver during practice sessions, but tonight he had an audience and he reacted to it.

Klatawah had been one of Dr. Carver's first diving horses. In the early years the horses had carried no riders, so in order to build up audience interest Dr. Carver had taught Klatawah to count out his age at the edge of the platform by pawing his hoof a number of times. Dr. Carver had long since wearied of this act (as had Al, since the pawing tore up the padding), but Klatawah had not; in fact, he thought it was splendid. He proceeded to count now by bringing first one foot and then the other high under his chin and letting them drop down with a whack that shook the very uprights.

The motion of his body as he went through these gymnastics jerked me backward and forward as if stricken with a violent case of hiccups. Klatawah was a fraud. He never actually counted his age; he simply pawed as many times as he thought the audience deserved, which could be a great number. Finally, however, he gave the audience one last look, then he clattered down onto the kickoff board with an almost running motion and immediately kicked off.

I felt his muscles tense as his big body sprang out and down, and then had an entirely new feeling. It was a wild, almost primitive thrill that comes only with complete freedom of contact with the earth. Then I saw the water rushing up at me, and the next moment we were in the tank.

We went in so smoothly that wetness seemed the only proof of landing. Klatawah's feet touched bottom and he began to nose up. I sensed a pull; the water parted; we came to the surface.

"I did it! I did it! I did it!" That was all I could think, and I was so excited when I dismounted that I forgot to bow to the audience. I simply turned and waved both arms, not once, but twice; it seemed the most natural thing in the world.

Then I turned to get Klatawah's sugar from the groom, but it wasn't the groom who was standing there. It was Dr. Carver, and he was smiling and said, "That's Daddy's girl."

Five

It was the first time he had ever called me "Daddy's girl," but I hardly heard him. I was too excited and full of myself. I went back to my dressing room, and in the mirror I saw I was grinning like a Cheshire cat. "What a pity," I thought, "there's no one to help me celebrate. I never felt so wonderful!"

The fact was that I hadn't a single friend in Durham. There might have been several reasons for this, but Dr. Carver was the overwhelming one. He didn't approve of my associating with people in the park; a top performer must maintain an air of mystery, he said. He was probably right, but just then I would have gladly traded mystery for some shared jubilation.

It wasn't until after I got back to the hotel that what he said really penetrated my mind. "That's Daddy's girl!" The only creatures who received this accolade were his beloved horses. If he had put me in the same category, our private war was over.

I was right in thinking that the title evidenced affection and pride, for he called me that in all the remaining years of our acquaintanceship, and because he liked it and because it seemed appropriate I called him "Daddy Carver." Many people took me for his daughter and I never bothered to correct them, for I became a daughter to him through devotion, if not by right of blood.

He had held off approval until I met the final test, afraid I might disappoint him somewhere along the way. I became convinced of this during the course of the next week when he started training a new girl for Al.

When Al left, Dr. Carver promised to send him a trained rider in time for his opening in Texas, and to that end had put an ad in the paper. The first applicant appeared just before matinee time three days after my initial ride from the high tower, and I was present when Dr. Carver explained the act and asked her to stay for the performance so she could see for herself. After the show she said she would like to try and was told to report the next morning.

For three mornings thereafter she was subjected to the same riding exercise I had undergone, but on the fourth Dr. Carver suddenly announced she was to make her first jump from the low tower.

As I went up on the platform with her to show her how to stand, I was deeply ashamed. I had spent weeks learning to hang onto the horse, and here she was riding from the low tower after only three days of ground training. I was not only ashamed but also perplexed. She had not ridden the horse any better than I had. What, then, did this mean?

The routine that followed after I came down from the tower was the same for her as it had been for me. The groom stopped the horse, she mounted, and after a brief pause the horse dived. I wasn't enough of a rider yet to judge, but since she was still on the horse when he came up I assumed she had done pretty well. Then she went up for the second time and the horse was turned into the runway, but the groom didn't release him after she had mounted. I could see that she was talking but could not hear what she was saying. From her gestures, however, I could tell that she was hesitating.

At this point the conversation on the tower was interrupted by Dr. Carver, who shouted, "What's going on there?" At that she threw both hands in the air, began screaming, and scrambled frantically over the horse's rump and down the incline.

I ran to the back of the tower. "What's the matter?" I asked, but she shot past me, unheeding, and slammed into the dressing room. About this time Dr. Carver walked up. "What happened?" I said.

"Nothing," he answered in disgust. "She just hasn't got the nerve."

"But," I argued, "maybe if you'd given her more ground training—"

"No," he said. "I haven't time to waste on a girl without nerve, and after watching her the past three mornings I decided she didn't have any. I let her ride from the tower just to be sure."

This, then, was the test. There had to be several along the way, and she had just flunked hers.

After we found someone to ride for Al, which we did the following week, we trained her and sent her off to Texas, and then there was nothing on our calendar except two daily performances. I passed the morning hours by practicing on the trap bar Al had put up for me before he left and by swimming in the tank. I was forbidden to swim in the big pool in the amusement park because Dr. Carver said that I shouldn't mix with my audience for the same reason I shouldn't mix with the people who worked in the park. "Familiarity breeds contempt," he said. "They've got to think you're special."

Thus I was forced into a close and isolated association with Dr. Carver. His influence was to prove to be both wide and deep, endowed with a creeping quality much like inflation. He influenced not only my deportment but also the length of my hair. I found to my astonishment that I was letting it grow!

In 1920 when I had cut my hair there were still precious few bobs in the South. Most women put their hair up or back but did not cut it. One day when I was sixteen I spent the afternoon with a friend, during the course of which we washed our hair. After the shampoo came the brushing and putting-up ritual, which always seemed to take hours. When I could not get my locks to stay in place because the pins kept sliding out, I suddenly reached for the scissors lying on Mamie Lou's dresser and hacked off my hair.

Within a minute it lay in a pile of red-brown glory, hair I had had since the day of my birth. There was silence, as well there might have been. I sat there looking at it, thinking, "Mother is going to kill me." Then I got up, pinned back what was left, and started to go home. I slipped in the back door and fled down the hall to the room I shared with Jac. When she came in later I buried my head in the pillow and pretended to be asleep.

The next morning I asked her to bring me the paper, planning to hide behind it and for a few minutes forestall the inevitable. I had hardly assumed a reading pose when I heard Mother coming down the hall. She threw open the door, stormed into the room, and snatched the paper out of my hands. Pointing to my head, she shouted, "I know!"

My little brother had seen me slinking home the night before and had made an announcement at breakfast. The upshot was that I was told to stay in the house until my hair grew long again. Such an order was out of the question, of course, and had to be rescinded, but for a long time Mother never looked at my shorn head without a disapproving and tormented sigh.

I took pride in my achievement and clung stubbornly to my bobbed hair. The fact was I liked it short. But in Durham I found myself with lengthening hair. Dr. Carver accomplished this by uncanny means. He said one day that he was pleased to see I was keeping my promise and letting my hair grow. I could not remember such a promise and I told him so. "Of course you did," he said firmly. So, on the basis of a statement that had no foundation in fact and certainly none in logic, Dr. Carver succeeded where my mother had failed.

Having won the victory with regard to my hair, he started in on my clothes. Women's dresses were beginning to creep up about that time and had reached a point three inches beneath the kneecap. This was shocking to Dr. Carver, who insisted that a "lady" never let her knees show, so whenever I went to buy a dress he came with me to make certain I got it long enough. If it didn't meet his standards he had it let down, and I ended up wearing hems about three or four inches longer than was fashionable.

On occasion I felt the old upward surge of defiance that was as much a part of me as my hands and feet, but I squashed it by asking myself, "What difference does it make? If it makes him happy, let him have his way."

My moments of antagonism were further salved by the fact that at least he was consistent. He was as strict with himself as he was with me and as conservative in his tastes. How it had happened that the flamboyant days of his youth had given way to such conservatism, I do not know. All I know is that his former love for the spectacular in clothing was now confined to a love for red, which he exhibited only in his ties.

However, he liked good clothes and paid a lot for them and took care of everything but his hats. These he sat on, crushed, abused, and, what was worse, wore no matter how they looked. He had only one for which he showed any reverence, though I never found out why. It was a white panama which he saved for special occasions.

In addition to conservative habits in dress, he never smoked or drank. In fact, he had never done either, even back in the old days, when to set a saloon door swinging was the hallmark of manhood. This was such a novelty that in time he became famous for his abstinence, and once when he was in St. Louis giving a shooting exhibition a group of women from the Women's Christian Temperance Union appeared and asked him to give public testimony to the fact that the reason he was so big and strong was that he never drank.

Dr. Carver refused. "I don't know that's why," he said. "Look at Buffalo Bill. He's just as big and strong and healthy as I am and he hasn't drawn a sober breath since I've known him. And that's been a long, long time."

His only vice was mild profanity. Life on the plains hadn't been designed to promote delicate speech, and his was not. The words were never foul, merely vigorous and forceful. They were also usually forgivable because he never realized he had used them. Once when I accused him of cursing he looked at me very hurt and said, "I *never* curse."

Where my language was concerned he would not permit even the mildest slang. "Gosh" and "golly" were not at all to his liking, nor "gee," "dern," or "darn." One day I thought I had found one that would surely get by without violating Dr. Carver's code. I had read it in the paper and anxiously awaited my chance to use it. It finally came one evening when we were sitting on the front porch of the boarding-house, talking to some people. Someone made a flat statement and I said, "Banana oil!"

Immediately Dr. Carver turned to me. "Haven't I told you *never* to use such language?" "Well," I said, "what in the world *can* I say?" He replied,

"You may say, 'Oh, my word.'" It occurred to me later that perhaps he wanted me to stay apart from other people not so much to provide an air of mystery as to keep me with him to see to his comforts. If this was so, it was too late by the time I caught on. I was too fond of him and too proud of his pride in me to take an independent stand.

That first summer was memorable principally for working with three of the horses. Lightning and John had gone off with Al and the new rider, but we kept Klatawah, Judas, and Snow.

Klatawah's name was Indian, meaning either "Go to hell" or "Go away," depending on the inflection. He was a chestnut sorrel gelding weighing about 1250 pounds, and his conformation was perfect. From stories I had heard, he had apparently been quite a devil in his younger days, but when I knew him he had settled down, which is not to say that he didn't have plenty of spirit; and he was the greatest showman of all the diving horses I have ever known.

He reminded me of a temperamental Shakespearean actor, the only difference being that a Shakespearean actor loves an intelligent audience and Klatawah loved a big one. His manner when working for a small crowd was so different as to make him seem two horses instead of one. When the crowd was small his whole body and every action seemed to radiate disgust. A person could almost feel his thoughts— "To think that I, Klatawah, the great diving horse—a star!—should be forced to work for such a miserable handful of people."

At such times he would flop over against the right side of the tower in a sort of reclining position, and instead of counting out his age vigorously at the edge of the platform, he would give vent to his disgust by making a few lazy scrapes at the pad, as if wiping his foot on a door mat. Then, more often than not, he would take off without bothering to straighten out of that absurd half-reclining position. This was hard on the rider, since it invariably caused a friction burn anywhere from the ankle to the knee, and I was forced finally to wear elastic ankle and knee bands to protect myself when I rode him.

Klatawah's style was the extreme plunge, which, according to definitions propounded by Dr. Carver, meant that when he took off he exerted the greatest pressure with his forelegs. This sent his body out in a lunging motion that was not as beautiful to watch as other diving styles, but Klatawah could make it spectacular because he worked with such fire.

The instant he realized the crowd was large he would begin to prance. Up would go the ears, and the beautiful arch in his neck would become more pronounced. When he worked like this the crowd always applauded with extra enthusiasm, and he loved the applause. In fact, as I was to learn later, he seemed actually to be jealous when another act got applause. Once while we were appearing in Atlantic City it was customary to bring the horses from their stables and keep them backstage until time for the dive. When the audience applauded an act working out front, the applause could be heard backstage. Klatawah would lift his head high in the air, listen intently, and then whinny, as if to say, "Just be patient. I'll be there."

The other types of dives horses made were the medium plunge, in which equal pressure is exerted with all four feet, a very graceful dive to witness; and the nose dive, which occurs when the horse exerts the greatest pressure with his hind feet. This last dive is not only very beautiful but also the most spectacular and by far the most difficult to ride.

In all three dives the horse enters the water head down and forelegs extended, but in the nose dive the horse enters the water with his whole body in an absolutely vertical position, while in the other two styles the body goes in at an angle. The extreme plunge was by far the easiest to ride, which was the reason I had learned on Klatawah.

There was more to Klatawah, however, than mere showmanship. He was utterly dependable and, aside from a real intelligence, had an endearing sense of duty. He first demonstrated this to me one day shortly after I had started diving from the high platform.

It was discovered just before performance time that the ground near the front of the tank had mired. When the workmen were preparing it they had scooped too much soil away from the incline and then back-filled with soft dirt to make up for their mistake. After a few days the slow seepage of water through the tarpaulin had turned the incline into a quagmire. Since this made it difficult for the horse to climb out, especially when burdened with a rider, Dr. Carver told me to dismount once we were in the water and let Klatawah swim out alone.

Ordinarily I would never have dismounted, since the mark of an expert rider is the one who stays with her horse, but that night as Klatawah surfaced I immediately let go and slipped off his back. When he started swimming he realized I was not on his back and turned and circled the tank, looking for me. He swam up beside me and gave me a look that clearly said, "You poor thing. Fell off, did you? Well, get back on. We've got to do this thing right, you know."

When I still did not mount but continued to do my own swimming he gave me another look which seemed to say, "Well, if that's the way you feel about it," and headed for the incline.

It would have been a different story with Judas. Judas, the horse I rode alternately with Klatawah, was, to put it bluntly, a horse of a different color. Had I slipped off his back while in the tank it is likely he would have gone off and let me drown. Not that he was malicious; he simply didn't care. For Judas it was every man for himself.

He was a white horse with roan ears and roan spots on his body. He had been given his name by a performer who was riding him on the practice lot one day when he threw her off over his head. "That horse is a Judas!" she had said, and Dr. Carver, overhearing, had seized on the name. He said that since he had one biblical character in the troupe—John the Baptist—he might as well have another.

Judas' personality contained more complex qualities than this streak of unreliability. Like many horses, he had an abundance of curiosity, and his was not only unusually strong but of a peculiar quality. It was the impersonal curiosity of a bystander, so completely cold-blooded that I had the feeling he would have stood by and watched any crime without turning a hair. Furthermore, his curiosity was so compelling that in his stall he never stood to eat his hay but after getting a mouthful would walk to the door and hang his head out. A lot of hay usually fell out of his mouth, and frequently as much as a third of his meal would end up outside on the ground, but Judas' philosophy seemed to be that he would rather satisfy his curiosity than his stomach. Later I became convinced that this animal was also capable of chagrin.

One day when he and Klatawah were out grazing in the pasture adjoining the tower I saw George going out to bring them back to the barn. It must have been a day when Judas was feeling unusually perverse, because the groom had no sooner led the two horses up to the barn than Judas suddenly cut to one side. The groom made a wild grab at his halter, but it was too late. Judas was off and away, and there was nothing for the groom to do but put Klatawah in his stall and then go back to get Judas.

By this time Judas must have decided to play a game. He stood perfectly still until the groom got close enough to reach his halter, then he threw back his head and took off. This happened four times, and each time the groom almost caught him. The fifth time, just as Judas jerked his head up, his hind feet skidded in a wet place on the lot and his hoofs dug a trench in a semicircle. In a half-up, half-down position he sat for a moment, then got up and with a completely crest-fallen appearance trotted back to the barn without the groom so much as laying a hand on him. George told me later that Judas went immediately to his stall and walked back to the farthest corner, where he stood with his face to the wall for the rest of the day.

Judas was a fair-to-middling diver, but he acquired a habit which, as time went on, developed beyond harmless eccentricity. Instead of standing on the floor of the tower to look the crowd over, he would drop down into position for the kickoff and simply hang there. At this point the strain on the arms and legs of the rider is severe, and the first few times he pulled this stunt my muscles felt as if they would relax in spite of me and that I would go off over his head. Finally one day I stretched my feet back to the padding on the tower and hooked my toes over the edge and, thus bracing myself, found I could remain on the edge just as long as he could.

While he hung there he seemed to be debating the merits of an extreme versus a medium plunge. Later, after many such indecisive poses, Judas invented a variation; he began to twist his body in mid-air after he took off and corkscrewed his way down, a trick that caused him to strike the water crosswise rather than toward the front of the tank. No one could guess what went on in his mind, but the maneuver seemed deliberate, since it took a great deal more physical effort to dive that complicated way. Deliberate or not, it held possibilities of real danger; he might hit the side of the tank or unseat the rider in mid-air. When we could not break him of his new habit, Dr. Carver reluctantly decided he must sell Judas.

He always hated to sell any of the horses, because he loved them in spite of their faults, but in Judas' case there seemed nothing else to do. The next step was to break him to the bridle and reins before seeking out prospective buyers. Each morning thereafter when Klatawah was taken to the parking lot to be exercised I went along on Judas to ride him back and forth.

In the beginning Judas exhibited a conspicuous lack of interest in being ridden and I was unable to get a real response from him, but one morning he was suddenly galvanized into action. "Well," I thought as he dashed off, "this is more like it." The groom was leading Klatawah back to the barn, and Judas, seeing his old friend, apparently wanted to tag along, hence the burst of speed. He must have decided almost simultaneously that he wished to carry me no farther, for he suddenly lowered his head, raised his hind feet, and made a little pig jump to one side. I did a complete somersault over his head and wound up sitting upright on the ground.

As I sat there, half dead, he galloped around me in a wide circle, taking care not to step in the dangling reins. The expression on his face, every movement of his body seemed to radiate silent amusement. It was as if he were saying, "Ha! Thought you were smart, didn't you, riding me that way. Now look at you. You're sitting in a puddle of mud." And I was. By some cunning he had contrived to dump me in the only muddy spot on the entire lot.

Switching my eyes from Judas to Dr. Carver, I found him doubled up laughing. "That horse is named right," I said. "I hope the person who buys him makes him pull a garbage wagon for the rest of his life." But Dr. Carver never sold him. When the chips were down, he couldn't bring himself to put an ad in the paper. Judas remained with us as a kind of pet— an expensive one—and Dr. Carver frequently berated himself for being softhearted. He would stop in front of Judas' stall and say, "I ought to sell that beggar. He doesn't do anything but eat."

The other horse we had with us that year was a mare named Snow. Her full name was Pure as Snow, which suited her perfectly. She was completely white, without a single colored hair on her whole body, nor was her skin marred by the dark blotches so often found on white horses. Had her weight been normal, her delicately shaped head and finely molded legs would have made a perfect model for a sculptor or painter, but unhappily Snow was a glutton.

In the beginning her gluttony had been a blessing, since she would do anything for a carrot and was therefore easy to train, but in the end it ruined not only her figure but her disposition.

In coaxing for bits of food she gradually evolved a routine that often ended in violence if she didn't get her way. First she would rub her nose on the door of her stall, then she would raise her foot and paw the air. Next she would raise her upper lip, as if smiling or laughing. If this fake cheerful countenance didn't get results, she would begin to kick her stall angrily and hard. She would have kicked it apart if Al had not reinforced it with extra planking.

Mealtime was the worst of all. Unless she was fed first she would simply go berserk, and even after she had been fed she would continue to fight savagely, kicking backward while she ate, as if she were afraid every horse in the barn was going to try to take her food away from her. Of course her continual weight gain ruined her for diving and she had to be retired, after which she was used only for breeding purposes.

The two remaining horses, Lightning and John, were with Al that season and I didn't ride either of them until the following year.

Six

We did not go directly into winter quarters my first year, as contracts had been signed for some midwinter fairs in Florida. The first and biggest was at Tampa, and from the time we got there I was all agog. I loved the booths in the lofty buildings with their exhibitions of bright-colored quilts and wine-red preserves and golden jars of honey, and I loved the smell of grain and hay in the stalls and the pen after pen of livestock. All this was magnified a dozen times at the South Florida Fair at Tampa, which was by far the biggest I had ever seen, and I was in a fever of excitement from the moment we arrived. During the morning hours Dr. Carver humored me; we walked aimlessly through the huge buildings crammed with everything from prune cake to pigeons, and one day during our wanderings I spied a litter of small red pigs just as the noonday sun was pouring through the windows, turning them into diminutive bits of animated fire. To my eager questions the attendant replied that they had been born that morning. I thought them cunning, so each day thereafter I insisted on going over for another look. Dr. Carver grumbled about being dragged "all over forty acres just to look at some damn pigs," but I was convinced then and still am that he enjoyed seeing them as much as I did.

For me that fair was special for another reason. Throughout the previous park and fair season the diving-horse act had been publicized in the newspapers. There had been pictures of the dive, and my name had appeared in stories on the pages devoted to theatrical news, but none of this had been personal. It had all been stock publicity material. Now at last there were reporters to interview me, and photographers took action pictures which were published in the leading Florida newspaper. Working beside me were people who were famous in the show world, but they didn't get the publicity our act received, which pleased me immensely. I was careful, however, not to get it in my head that I was a big shot. I knew that it was the act the people came to see, not me, and that it had been the outstanding act of the business long before my time.

The term "free act" perhaps needs some explanation. A free act is one that is put on as a special attraction at amusement parks and fairs in order to draw a crowd. It is not, as some people assume, an act that performs free.

The term was coined back in the old days when harness racing was popular. Track managers were hard put to keep the audience occupied, until someone came up with the idea of getting professional performers to entertain during these intervals. The professionals at first were garnered from the circus, and their acts were called "free acts" because no fee was added to the usual cost of admission.

Later acts were evolved for the special purpose of performing at harness races, acts that had never been and never were part of the circus. Gradually these acts moved away from race tracks into the world of the country or state fair as well as that of the amusement parks. Dr. Carver was astute enough to spot a trend and pioneered in the training of diving horses for the specific purpose of appearing as a free act all over the country.

By the time spring came Lorena had recovered sufficiently from her leg surgery to be able to ride, so it was she who left with Al when he went out in April to open at the Old Spanish Fort Park in New Orleans. This was fortunate, since Anne, the girl Dr. Carver had hired and trained in Durham the spring before, had turned out to be a poor performer. From Al's point of view as a showman, she had proved to be a dud by committing the unforgivable crime of climbing off Lightning's back onto the framework of the tower just as the horse was ready to dive. Though it had been only a temporary loss of nerve, it happened on two occasions, and in Al's opinion she was all washed up.

Both he and his father put a great deal of stock in courage. Neither of them had any use for anyone without it; at least not anyone who wanted to ride. In so far as having nerve was concerned, I suppose I had it, but if I did it was no credit to me, since it was as natural to me as fingernails.

Having courage is, I think, like having money. If a man who has a million dollars walks down the street and sees some valuable article in a shopwindow that he wants to buy, he goes in and buys it without any thought of what it costs, but if a man without any money sees the same article and feels the same desire to own it he immediately realizes he can't have it because he hasn't the money. The point is, if you have it you don't think about it, but if you don't have it the realization is often thrust upon you.

Actually, true courage is what it takes to make yourself do something you're afraid to do. I was not afraid of riding the horses; on the contrary, I loved it and would not have given it up willingly. In the beginning I loved it because I adored the horses and liked traveling around the country, but later the crowds were an added factor. The wolf whistles that followed me up the ramp, the applause that burst out spontaneously as I climbed to the top, the call of the clown in the audience who shouted, "Hold 'er, Newt, she's a-rarin'"— these were the people for whom I performed; good-natured, responsive, admiring. I loved them all. But this stage passed; more and more as time went by I discovered I wasn't riding for their applause. I was riding for the sheer animal thrill I got every time we cleared the tower.

The physical, wholly sensual pleasure that comes with the drop from the tower down to the tank is a pleasure totally lacking in psychological or philosophical meaning. It's the sheer exhilaration of being entirely free of the earth as well as everything human; to me no other physical sensation can be so acute, so deeply intoxicating.

Did I also enjoy flirting with death? It never seemed to me that that was what I was doing, though in fact I was. Had I been conscious of this I would probably have quit, since I have too much common sense to keep on doing something that I feel will end in anything quite so irrevocable and final. But then I suppose we are all great believers in our own immortality; death can happen to others but surely not to us.

The year after Al and Lorena left for New Orleans, Dr. Carver and I went to Kansas City to appear at Fairmont Park for the season, and this time we traded horses. Al took Klatawah and Snow and Judas, and we kept Lightning and John.

Lightning was our largest horse, weighing some fifteen hundred pounds. Her name had been Babe when purchased, but this wasn't nearly ostentatious enough for either her or show business. Dr. Carver renamed her

"Lightning" because of the speed with which she worked. Some years later he added the title "Duchess" in honor of a real duchess who happened to be visiting a town in Canada when the act was working there. The duchess saw Lightning and tried to buy her. Dr. Carver refused to sell, but he did change her name. From then on she became officially "The Duchess of Lightning," although in conversation we never called her anything but "Lightning."

In spite of her name, however, she was more terrified in bad weather than any animal I have ever known, and whenever there was a thunderstorm we had to make certain someone she loved was with her. At other times she was the bravest of all the horses. If anything frightened them while in the pasture she would dash off with the others, but she invariably returned first to see what had caused the excitement. She would stand stiff-legged blowing through her nostrils, head up and ears back, before turning to scamper off again.

Although Lightning lacked most of those personality quirks that made the other horses so entertaining, she had one characteristic I have always adored in a horse. She talked to people with little whinnies and nickers. When one of us went into the stables at night it was always she who called out, sometimes in such a human way that it seemed as if she summoned us by name. This gentle friendliness was very touching, and I shall never forget the day I was forced to hurt her feelings.

It was a Sunday and Dr. Carver had decided to give the audience an extra treat by having both horses dive instead of only one. He therefore arranged for Lightning to make a dive alone and for me to follow immediately, riding John. When the time came he sent Lightning up ahead of me, in place of my preceding her, as was the usual routine. Although all the horses except Snow had been trained to dive with or without a rider, Lightning really preferred to have a passenger. That Sunday when she got to the top and I wasn't there she looked around for me.

I had just started up the ramp behind her, planning to get into place after her dive, but when she saw me coming she apparently assumed she should wait. I climbed onto the railing and made no move to mount her; she gave me a look that was clearly puzzled and then backed up. She looked at me as if to say, "Is that better? Am I standing right? Can you get on from here?"

I saw there was nothing to do but force her off the platform, so I reached out and slapped her smartly on the rump. She took off almost immediately, but not before giving me one last look full of reproach. I felt a deep sense of guilt at not being on her back where she wanted me.

Of the five animals, John was unqualifiedly the most amusing—"a real character." A big horse, our biggest next to Lightning, he weighed some fourteen hundred pounds. He was light brown, with almost roan ears and roan spots on his body. John was the smoothest diver among the horses and was also an excellent swimmer, although he preferred to make you believe otherwise.

For some reason, he didn't like bringing a rider out of the tank, although he was certainly big and strong enough. As a result he always tried to unseat a newcomer (and sometimes the veterans as well) by putting on an act. After making a dive, instead of heading for the incline with a series of powerful, rhythmic strokes as he did when behaving himself, he would remain in one spot, thrashing the water with strokes so feeble that he was barely able to keep his head above water. By his actions he seemed to be saying, "Look, I'm not strong enough to carry you while I swim, so please be a good girl and get off."

If this appeal to pity failed, he would then change his tactics so suddenly as to make it obvious that he had been faking all along. He would bring his forefeet to the surface and begin pawing the air until he rolled over on his side or back. With some girls this maneuver had the desired effect, for they would turn loose and head for shore, leaving John to right himself and swim out, wearing a very smug expression.

Dr. Carver had warned me about his tricks in advance, telling me not to get off, that he was only bluffing and I wasn't to let him get away with it. The first time I rode John I stuck with him even after he rolled over. Since that took a little doing, I decided to outsmart him the next time by trying a trick of my own. As soon as his forefeet appeared after the dive, I dismounted but still retained a grip on the harness with one hand, and John, feeling my weight gone, thought he was rid of me and began swimming strongly for the incline. At this point I slid into position on his back and rode him out in triumph.

The last time he tried the rolling-over trick on me was one night when he floundered all over the tank while I alternately mounted and dismounted until we were against the back wall. There, realizing he was fighting a losing battle, John suddenly straightened up and headed for the incline with such speed and precision as to amaze the spectators, who had been certain he was drowning.

He had a very stubborn streak and, once he set his mind on anything, it was impossible to change it. That year in Kansas City the diving structure was built beside a big tree, the branches of which brushed the right side of the tower. The branches had some delicious new green leaves on them, and John spotted them right away. Lightning was too much of a lady to eat leaves in public, but John wasn't about to ignore anything so appetizing. On his first trip up the ramp he came to a halt and took a bite. He then went to the front of the platform, where he finished chewing before making his dive. The audience found this byplay delightful, but we were afraid to let him continue munching on the leaves for fear he might dive before he had swallowed and thus run the risk of strangling. The next night, when he made a grab at a branch, I jerked his head back before he reached his goal, but that didn't discourage him. After another try in the same direction which I also prevented, he suddenly swivelled around, snatched a mouthful, and then leaped off the platform. Fortunately he didn't strangle. Dr. Carver had the limb cut off the next morning.

Anything at all unusual attracted John's attention, and he invariably tried to investigate. Once while experimenting with a new system of lighting for the tower, bulbs were placed on the outer edges of the apron. Lightning paid no attention to them, but John immediately became interested in one particular globe, the top one on the left. On the right was another just as bright and a whole lot closer, but that seemed to make no difference to him.

Each time just before he dived he tried to reach the bulb with his left foot but failed. Finally one night after he was already in a diving position it seemed as though he couldn't endure being frustrated any longer, for he suddenly pulled back up on the tower and with his right foot reached over his left and put his roof down on the globe. The bulb burst with a loud explosion that startled John (and me) into the world's fastest take-off.

Another time when we were working a fair in Massachusetts the man who had charge of decorations placed additional streamers of colored lights on our tower. These streamers, extending from the top of the tower to the ground, provided John with a new toy. He didn't make a single dive at night during the whole fair that he didn't reach over and bump a streamer with his nose. Of course this caused all the lights to vibrate. He would watch the vibration intently until it died away, and then he would nudge the streamer again. He formed a habit of nudging the lights three times before each dive.

Apparently he had a good deal of judgment, whatever his eccentricities, for he often used discerning faculties not usually found in a horse. Later that season, after we had left Fairmont, our tower and tank were set up facing a lake about a thousand yards away. The first two or three times John dived he couldn't seem to figure it out. He would look down at the diving tank, which must have seemed awfully small in comparison with the lake, and after a moment's intense consideration of it he would then raise his head and stare fixedly at the lake. This would continue, first the tank and then the lake, several times before he dived; he seemed to be wondering why he had to dive into anything so small when there was all that water out there.

Aside from having better than average brains, he was a mischief-maker and a tease and annoyed the other horses constantly when they were out in the pasture. One day he came up with a new trick, the wonder of which was that he thought it up himself. He made off with the broom that was standing beside the bam door and galloped out to the pasture where the other horses were grazing. He dashed at them with the broom between his teeth, brandishing it as he ran, which of course sent them off in a panic. This seemed to please John enormously and he continued chasing them around until he finally tired of the game and dropped the broom.

It was with these two splendid animals, Lightning and John, that we ended the season at the Essex County Fair in Topsfield, Massachusetts, where extensive advertising had given the diving horses top billing. As a result we faced a battery of newsreel cameras. After that we appeared in news-reels many times and also made some short subjects, but the first time for anything is always the most exciting, and I've always remembered Topsfield with affection.

Seven

The summer of 1926, spent at Krug Park in Omaha, Nebraska, was uneventful aside from one incident, an incident memorable because it was my first experience with a near-serious mishap.

One Sunday afternoon just as John was about to dive, the harness suddenly came loose. He brought up short at the head of the platform, and I shot off over his head. As I fell I caught hold of a handful of mane and hung there suspended forty feet in the air.

It was not the height that created my danger, however. I could easily have let go and dropped, but I was afraid that if I did the horse would dive in on top of me.

Al was with us at the time and he shouted from below, "Let go! Let go and drop!" But I knew it would be safer to get back on the platform.

In the midst of all the commotion John stood in calm bewilderment, feet set, neck bowed, jaw taut and firm. "I'll go off this thing right," he seemed to say, "but I'll be darned if you're going to pull me off."

This attitude was exactly what I needed. Since he was set so firmly, I could swing my body up and get my feet on the padding, after which I was able to get hold of an upright and pull myself onto the platform.

When I told Al later why I hadn't let go, he said, "That's using your head. I was so excited I never even thought about it. There are three things a good rider has got to have —steady nerves, the ability to think quickly, and the ability to act quickly. You've got all of them. Every rider is going to get her share of bruises and bumps, but the good one is the one who can make instantaneous decisions and act on them. People think that in this business you don't have to have any brains. They're wrong. The first time you stop thinking, you're dead."

Al didn't bother to hide the fact that he didn't think many people had brains. He was short-tempered and cocky and frequently untactful. He suffered from the overbearing ways of his father, as all of us did, but the main trouble between father and son was that they were too much alike. Al, who had real ability and his own brand of showmanship, had to knuckle down constantly, which seldom set well. When he was away he could do pretty much as he pleased, but when he was with us in winter quarters or occasionally during the season, it was a different story. Such times he accepted his father's domination, but there was anger beneath the acceptance, and this he usually unleashed as soon as his father was out of sight.

Lorena did not suffer at Dr. Carver's hands perhaps because she was a daughter, and daughters seem to be provided with fatherly exemption. Still, she must have learned from past experience not to cross him, which probably was not always easy, for she too had a strong will of her own.

An especially trying time for Al occurred each year when we got organized for the season. He always packed Dr. Carver's trunks and despised every minute of the process, because Dr. Carver would sit by and insist upon telling Al exactly where to put everything, whether it fit or not. To suggest an alternate arrangement proved altogether useless, because at that point Dr. Carver acted as if his son were about six years old and couldn't possibly know what he was talking about.

After witnessing several of these sessions I volunteered to take over the packing, and Al relinquished it with a sigh of relief. When the minute supervision threatened to barricade progress, I learned to get around it by overemphasizing the fact that an object wouldn't fit; I exaggerated the fruitless effort of forcing it in. After a pause I would say, "I think your first suggestion was best."

To this he would look thoughtful, as if trying to recall what he had proposed; then he would say, "Let's see. What was it?"

Of course I would proceed to pack according to my own ideas. The diplomatic approach proved to be the only way to handle Dr. Carver.

The accident with John took place the week before Labor Day, and a week later the amusement-park season closed. Once again summer had gone and it was time to make the fall fairs. We were scheduled for two that fall, the second being the country fair at Lexington, North Carolina. It was here that my most humiliating experience as a rider took place.

We were due to open the night of October 7, but Dr. Carver, who had a cold and wanted to go to bed early, asked Al and Lorena to do the act in our place. I retired to my room with a book.

Just at performance time Al appeared at my door. Lorena's leg, he said, had begun to bother her again and she didn't think she should make the dive. Al asked me to take her place.

It was my first sight of the Lexington fairgrounds, and the strange surroundings plus the sense of hurry made me feel a little dizzy as I got into my suit and put on my shoes.

Al had taken particular pains to point out that I would ride the horse out of the tank; why, I do not know, since he didn't ordinarily. Maybe it was to give me a pat on the back. I had ridden 165 times by then and not fallen off once. "Gotten knocked off" is really a more apt expression, since that is what happens, but anyway you say it, the fact remains that I had stayed with my horse and was proud of my record.

Whether it was the hurry, the unfamiliarity of the park, or inner nervousness, I do not know, but when Klatawah hit the water I found myself floating free and coming up at the side of the tank. Someone reached out a hand to help me; I caught hold of it and pulled myself out of the water.

I wasn't hurt, but my pride had just suffered a terrible blow. I wanted to be a perfect rider more than anything else and I had just proved I was not. I was so downcast I didn't even bother to bow to the audience and afterward, on the way home, got quite a tongue-lashing from Dr. Carver, who had gotten out of bed to go down with us.

"You were showing off," he said. "That's the reason it happened. You weren't paying any attention to the business at hand. Always think about what you're doing. Furthermore," he added ominously, "I don't care what happens to you out there, whether you get hurt or fall off or what—you bow to that audience and smile and wave just as if nothing had gone wrong. The place for groaning or for being embarrassed is in the dressing room. Never let the audience suspect that you have failed or been injured. That's part of showmanship."

Al's complaint was that it had to be *that* time I'd fallen off. "Any other time," he said, "I wouldn't even have mentioned that you were going to ride the horse out of the tank. But no, I play it up and what happens? You fall off!"

It taught me a valuable lesson other people had discovered before me. As someone aptly put it, "Pride goeth before a fall."

When we had finished the fair Dr. Carver gave the order to strike the platform and take the canvas out of the tank. I liked to watch this process. Instead of draining the pool and then taking out the canvas, the men removed the canvas while the water was still in it. They first untied the ropes from around the stakes and unfastened the stakes from the grommets. Then they worked the tarp forward until it was away from the wall, letting some water go behind it to make the canvas float to the surface. Then they pumped it up and down, forcing air under it until it began to balloon up. It took six or eight men to pull it out, since it was very large and very heavy when wet. Once they had it out, they stretched it on the ground to dry and afterward folded it up to be shipped.

This time was no different from any other, except that a little turtle came riding along on top of the canvas. How he had wandered into the tank nobody could guess, but there he was, no bigger than the palm of a hand and a truly beautiful specimen. His olive-green back was ornamented with a design resembling a dray, leafless brown twig. The shell underneath was a bright salmon pink and had the same twiglike design but in olive green and brown. His feet, legs, neck and head were striped in vivid hues of green and yellow. I had seen many turtles in aquariums and other places, but never one like him.

Dr. Carver loved the small creatures and had often entertained me with anecdotes about them, but at the time he had no pet, so he adopted the turtle and named him "King Tut." For the first day or two after we found him King Tut remained tightly encased in his shell, but constant handling without injury must have created confidence, for eventually he trudged about the floor with all the familiarity of a creature in its native environment. One day, however, Dr. Carver forgot he was on the floor and accidentally stepped on him. I was in another room when I heard the bellow, "Where's Daddy's girl?" and immediately I went running because I could hear the fright in his voice. I found him holding Tut and looking badly shaken. "I stepped on him!" he said hoarsely. "And look what I did!"

I took Tut and examined him and found that the seams of the shell had been cracked on the right side by not actually crushed. I hadn't the least idea what to do with a fractured turtle, but I knew I had to do something. I took him to the bathroom, put iodine on the break and bound it over with adhesive tape. About a week later when we removed the bandages there wasn't a trace of the injury.

We were ready to leave for Tampa and winter quarters again. Dr. Carver found a little box for the turtle, put him in it, and calmly boarded the train.

In the middle of the night I felt someone shaking my shoulder. "Wake up!" he said. "I've lost Tut. You've got to come find him."

I slipped into my dressing gown and followed Dr. Carver back to his berth.

"How in the world did you lose him?" I asked.

"When I woke up," he said, "and couldn't get back to sleep I took him out of his box to keep me company. In some way he must have slipped down between the bed and the wall of the car."

I scoured his berth for the turtle, shaking out sheets and peering under it, but Tut was not there. Obviously there was nothing for it but to get down on my hands and knees and crawl along the aisle, peering under each berth. I tried to see behind luggage by pushing and tugging. I pulled socks and stockings out of an endless assortment of shoes, patiently shaking out each one and hoping that the lost creature would reappear. As I searched I frantically racked my brain for a plausible excuse for my actions in case some passenger should wake and ask me what I was doing.

Down one side and up the other I crawled, but still there was no Tut. Just as I reached the end where the corridor curved around the ladies' washroom, I met him, silhouetted against the dim light of the morning. Apparently his tour had been blocked by the door at the end of the car and he was returning to the main part of the car. As I picked him up I couldn't help wondering just how much of a hullabaloo would have been created if some squeamish woman on her way to the washroom had met him.

When we were settled in Tampa, I began on the letters concerning the next season's bookings and also took on Dr. Carver's personal correspondence.

He had a set of old cronies dating back to his days on the plains. Most of the time he was too busy to correspond with them, or declared that he was. Actually, like many people, he enjoyed getting letters but procrastinated when it came to replying. That winter it occurred to him that he had me as a typist and began to write with renewed vigor.

One of the old-timers he kept up with was Dr. Richard Tanner, known in his days on the plains as "Diamond Dick." Early in 1927 he wrote Dr. Carver that he had learned that the Newspaper Editors Association of America was planning a western tour in June and would be passing through Norfolk, Nebraska, where Dr. Tanner had settled down to the practice of medicine. He and some of his friends had hit on the idea of inviting the editors to stop off there to attend an Old-Timers' Convention. He wanted to know if Dr. Carver could come.

Dr. Carver had me write immediately that he'd be there. He loved nothing better than talking over the old days with his friends. He had signed a contract for a season's engagement at Lick's Pier in Ocean City, California, which was to begin the first week in June, but he said he would send Al and Lorena to open there and we would follow later.

The eager anticipation with which Dr. Carver looked forward to the celebration reminded me of a small boy getting ready to go to his first circus. He had neither worn a big hat nor ridden a horse since he sold all of his Wild West show paraphernalia in 1911 and gone into the free-act business, but now he ordered an oversized hat directly from the Stetson company and had his saddle washed and polished. The saddle, appraised at ten thousand dollars, was a collector's item, decorated with intricately etched silver and ornamented with silver coins which he had pierced with rifle bullets in the presence of the notables of Europe during his shooting career.

Having taken care of the externals, we left Tampa for Norfolk, Nebraska. On June 12 the convention opened and many of the old-timers who were still living were there: Diamond Dick, Pawnee Bill, Deadwood Dick, Captain North, Idaho Bill, and Evil Spirit (Dr. Carver). They spent every available minute together, and Dr. Carver had a wonderful time. When it was over, much too soon as far as he was concerned, we went to Omaha, where he had some business with a museum. It was while we were there that he received a telegram.

LIGHTNING INJURED. SUGGEST YOU COME AS SOON AS POSSIBLE. LETTER FOLLOWS.

AL

He was more upset than I had ever seen him before. "Oh, my horse! My pretty horse!" he kept repeating. "I should have know something like this was going to happen. I had a dream about a month ago in which Lightning was hurt. Oh, my pretty horse!"

Worse was to come, however, and it came with Al's letter:

The day after Lorena and I arrived here in California, I went out to take a look at the setup. As you know, I never liked the idea of diving the horses into the ocean, but since we had signed a contract to that effect I decided I'd better find out how they were going to react So the next day I took John out and put him through his paces.

He went in like a trouper and turned around and headed for the shore. The breakers near shore were hard for him to pull against and ended up turning him head over heels and buffeting him around until he could reach shallow water and get his footing. Still, he made it and I hoped that he and the other horses would become accustomed to the ocean. The next day I tried Lightning.

She made a beautiful dive, but when she saw how rough the breakers were she apparently attempted to find an easier way out. The horse swam around the end of the pier and disappeared under some pilings. I ran over and looked under the pier but couldn't see her. Then she was spotted heading out toward the open sea, and some lifeguards jumped in a boat and started out after her. Lightning glanced behind her at the boat and seemed to react to the rescuers by swimming even harder and faster. She completely outdistanced them for a while but before long began to tire. As I was watching from the shore, she gave up—put her head down and drowned.

The lifeguards secured a rope around her neck and towed her back to the beach. By the time they arrived we had a pulmotor ready, but it wasn't any use. Lightning was already gone.

Of course I already knew all this when I wired you but wanted to break the news as gently as possible. I thought that the wire might prepare you a little.

I have called off the contract until you can get here. We certainly don't want to risk losing another horse and I think you will agree. . . .

I had been reading the letter aloud to Dr. Carver, and as I did so my voice thickened until I was forced to break off. I looked at him tearfully and saw that the ridges between his eyes had deepened as they always did under stress. Then he looked at me and said sadly, "Go pack your things."

Eight

We took the first train west and, when we got to Ocean Park, Dr. Carver canceled the contract. From that moment on life seemed to go out of him, as if it were visibly ebbing. He was eighty-seven by then and it was time for him to be tired, but it was more than a physical tiredness; it was a weariness of the heart.

Having canceled the contract, there was nothing for us to do until our next scheduled appearance at the California State Fair in Sacramento the first week in September. We took rooms in a hotel in Ocean Park and prepared to wait out the summer.

If Dr. Carver had been dependent on me before, he was doubly so now. He did not wish me out of his sight for more than a few moments. I had long since sacrificed personal friendship to his demands, but now the demands included even the stray bits of time that had formerly been mine. When I wanted to do such a simple thing as walk down to the beach a few blocks away and take a swim he wouldn't let me. He was like a child afraid of the dark and, seeing how upset he was, I stayed with him all the time.

Then one day, out of the blue, he told me to call Al because he wanted to talk to him about taking over while we went on a trip. He had decided that he wanted me to see Yosemite. We could still get back, he said, in plenty of time to make the fair at Sacramento.

I was so pleased to see him begin to come out of his shell that I agreed instantly. I called Al, they made their plans, and a few days later we left. But while we were stopping off at Merced, where Dr. Carver had some old friends he wanted to see, his feet began to swell. When he called me to help him put on his shoes, I was alarmed at the swelling and told him I was going to call a doctor.

"Oh no, you're not! I don't want any doctors around here!" He reacted so violently that I decided to wait. However, when the swelling had not gone down by the next day and, in fact, seemed to be worse, he gave in and reluctantly agreed to medical attention.

The doctor who came to his hotel room and examined him said, "You shouldn't be traveling around like this. Where do you live?"

"I live where I am," Dr. Carver replied. "That's where I live."

"Well, you'll have to go to the hospital then," the doctor said. "I'll make the arrangements."

"The devil you will!" Dr. Carver thundered. "I'm not going to any damn hospital."

Taken aback, the doctor did not press further. Evidently he felt it was hopeless and decided to save himself trouble. At the door he gave me a prescription and some whispered advice: "His heart is going back on him. Make him stay in bed or, better yet, get him somewhere permanent and keep him quiet."

I shook my head and he smiled at me. "I know, nobody can manage that kind, but do the best you can."

He had no sooner left than Dr. Carver called me to him and told me to put on his shoes.

"But the doctor said—"

"The hell with the doctor. I'm going down to the lobby." And with this he leaned over and began grappling with the shoes, so that of course I had to help him.

Downstairs he took a seat on one side of the lobby and proceeded to glower at everyone. He finally fixed his attention on a group of women, most of whom were smoking. "Silly bunch of idiots!" he said. "Don't they know how unladylike they look?" After he had snorted and growled until he wore himself out he went back upstairs.

To my great relief, the rest and medicine helped, and in a few days he insisted upon continuing the trip to Yosemite. I thought perhaps it would take his mind off himself, so I agreed, but his condition was so constantly on my mind that I don't remember much about Yosemite. In fact, we had no sooner arrived there than I became very uneasy and determined to get back. Just as soon as I could persuade him I had enough of the park, we left for Sacramento.

Lorena and Al met us at the station, and after we got to the hotel I took them aside and told them what had happened to their father. We agreed that he should be persuaded to settle down and let Al handle the act, but we also agreed that it was highly unlikely he would go along with this scheme.

Dr Carver seemed to feel pretty well the first few days we were back, but one afternoon he suddenly became so ill he had to go to bed. Still he wouldn't let me get a doctor. The next morning he seemed even worse, and when I insisted I was going to call a doctor he didn't put up a fight.

The doctor came and repeated the first doctor's diagnosis and also firmly suggested taking him to the hospital. Although Dr. Carver was lying in bed with his eyes closed, to all appearances not listening, at the word "hospital" his eyes popped open. "No damn hospital," he said, and immediately closed them again.

The doctor gave me a prescription and said in that case there was nothing more he could do.

He came every day for three or four days after that, and Dr. Carver seemed to get better. As a matter of fact, by the end of the week he was sitting up, joking with some friends who had dropped by, but the recovery was a false one. That night he got worse. He was sick all night and by morning seemed so exhausted that when the maid came to change his linens I told her not to bother him, but he heard me whispering and opened his eyes. "Let her," he said, and, raising himself, threw one of the blankets around himself and walked a few steps across the room to a chair. When he sat down I looked at his face and knew as I had not known before that he was going to die.

It hit me so hard that I almost cried out, but I held onto myself and, telling the maid to call me when she was through, hurried to my room. There I stayed and had my cry.

When I returned I helped him out of the chair and back into bed, and that night he lapsed into a coma. In the morning we took him to the hospital, but he didn't even know. He had had a long and eventful trip through life, but the end had come at last. Dr. Carver died that afternoon.

We could not go with him to his final resting place. He died only three days before we were to open in Sacramento, and he had told us, "No matter what happens to me, don't break any contracts. My word has always been good and I want to keep it that way." So we sent him off alone to a grave beside his parents in Winslow, Illinois, knowing he would have wanted it that way and that we were doing the thing he would have most respected; we were keeping his word.

I tried to keep busy after that, getting ready for our appearance. Because of Dr. Carver's illness I hadn't had time to buy any new bathing suits. I went out and bought a dozen in different colors and styles and also some spangles to sew on those I'd be wearing at night. This was a wide departure from the outfits I had worn before, but now I was working for Al, and Al's outlook was different from his father's. He allowed his performers to dress the way they pleased, so I put away forever the old red suit with its modest neckline and gave over to a new magnificence.

To top my new finery, Lorena gave me a shawl of green silk with long fringe around the edge and a peacock on the back. She had embroidered the peacock herself with a large punch-work needle, and I was as thrilled when I had it on as a little girl dressed up in her mother's finery.

In one last gesture of putting aside the old and taking up the new, I discarded the helmet. For a long time Lorena had not worn one when she was away from her father, adopting in its place a headpiece made of sateen over a regular bathing cap. Surely by this time, I told myself, I had been diving long enough to know how to protect myself from the horses' hoofs.

There was one thing I couldn't bring myself to change. Dr. Carver had been so pleased when I let my hair grow—"Now you look like a lady"—that for a long time I refused to cut it.

The night we opened in Sacramento it was Al who announced the act. He pulled out all the stops, and the spiel he unwound was a sure guarantee to make everyone listening believe he was about to witness the most breathtaking performance in history.

"Ladies and gentlemen," Al said, "all eyes cast atop this lof-ty tower," breaking the word "lofty" in such a way as to make it seem as high as any human could possibly go without benefit of oxygen. "Tonight we present for your entertainment the most exciting act in show business today ..." and so on until every eye was hopelessly and completely glued to the tower.

Al had picked up his art of announcing in his days with the circus he had run away to join when he was only eleven. Eleven years old and a runaway, a dead match for his father; yet his reason for running had not been the same. He had not been mistreated; he had been ignored. It was during the time his father owned a Wild West show and Al yearned to go touring with the cowboys and Indians, but Dr. Carver forbade it, saying he wanted Al to stay home with his mother and go to school. Al simply up and left home.

With an eleven-year-old's impracticality he chose the month of December, which, living in Colorado as he did, was the next thing to suicide. He caught a freight train leaving Colorado Springs for Denver just as it pulled out of the yard, but he didn't climb up inside a boxcar because he was too small to catch hold. Instead he crawled onto the cowcatcher, whose big underslung iron jaw jutted out in front of the engine, and it was here that he spent the night.

He might have been all right had it not started to snow. By the time he reached Denver he was nearly frozen and in fact probably would have been if the yard men who checked the cars had not found him asleep on the cowcatcher.

In Denver he became a Jack-of-all-trades. He couldn't join the circus right away because it was winter. Also, he knew his father would look for him among show people.

He began by going to work for a construction company as a lantern boy. It was his job to trim the wicks of the lanterns and fill them with coal oil each day for use out on the job each night

Next he worked in a butcher shop delivering meat. As it happened, the butcher had a sickly wife who often solicited Al's help in the kitchen when she was too ill to prepare the meal herself, and in that way Al soon learned to cook.

The following summer he figured enough time had elapsed to make it safe for him to join the circus. When it came to Denver he found a job with a woman bareback rider. It became his duty to feed and water the horses and otherwise make himself useful.

When he wasn't helping her he was free to help anyone else on the lot who needed him. He often managed to be free in time to perform the most coveted tasks, feeding and watering the elephants and assisting the roustabouts set up the tents. In reminiscing he said that far and away his biggest thrill came the day he got to drive a circus wagon.

It was a big twelve-horse team that pulled a cage of tigers. The driver had taken ill suddenly and someone was needed to take his place. Al was handy and willing even if he was small, so they turned the wagon over to him, and when he climbed up on the box he says he never felt so magnificent. His hands weren't big enough to hold the reins for that many horses, but he was smart enough not to admit it. He simply knotted half of them together and wound them around a stanchion, after which he proceeded to guide the team with the other half. He then drove down Main Street to the music of the calliope and the circus band and gazed down on the hundreds of unfortunate school children who had not had the good sense to run away and join the circus.

He was with the circus about five years, and during that time he did everything from bareback riding to selling tickets to announcing the acts.

Al was nineteen when he decided to leave the circus and go around the world. By this time, of course, Dr. Carver had long since located his wandering son and given up trying to persuade him to go back to school. When Al returned from a world cruise (glad to be on land again after a typhoon), his father taught him to train horses for the diving act, which was a natural for Al with his circus background. After Dr. Carver's death it wasn't long before people in the business were referring to Al as "Doc" the way they had his father and looking to him for the same high-caliber performance his father had always provided. Thus the voice that announced me that night in Sacramento may have been different, but the regime was not.

Nine

Because we had been late getting started, the season passed very quickly, but for the first time since I had joined the troupe we did not go to Florida in the fall. Al and Lorena decided that we would go instead to Lorena's farm in Bucks County, Pennsylvania.

For years Al had fumed about the cost of transportation. "All we do," he said, "is make money one place so we can take it down and hand it over to the railroad so they can take us someplace else." His fuming was justified, because fares did cost a fortune. Dr. Carver would not consider traveling any way but first class, and it took half a freight car for our horses. Now, however, there were beginning to be good highways across the country and Al decided that the time had come to buy a car and save money. He had to compromise by allowing the horses to travel by train but insisted he would do so only until he could have a truck built for them to his own specifications.

The first car he bought was a Chevy with a rumble seat. Rumble seats were all the rage then, seeming to represent the wind-blown freedom which had come with the twenties. The cartoon of a shingled head over the top of a rumble seat with a flask uptilted was quite a common one but, as far as I was concerned, overdone. There were flappers and there were speakeasies and jazz and short dresses and cigarettes, but all these were part of the big cities—the East mainly— not the small towns I had grown up in. I had been in many big cities since I left home, but Dr. Carver had quashed any inclination I might have had toward revolution. The twenties might have been roaring, but I didn't hear the roar.

The fact was, I was too sensible for things like rumble seats. As far as I could see, they weren't good for anything but to mess up my hair. Fortunately Al and Lorena felt the same way, so the Chevy didn't last long. Al sold it within a short time and bought a Studebaker Big 6 Special. The top was leather, the windows rolled up and down, and it had wire wheels. We were all set to travel across the country in style when it was discovered that by the time all three of us got our trunks and suitcases in the back and Lorena got her Pekinese and the binoculars and the candy and the crackers in there wasn't room for people. Realizing that at best it would be uncomfortable on long cross-country trips, Al went out and bought a second car, defending the purchase by declaring that from now on we would have to have two anyway since there would still be two separate units touring the country. Lorena was going to take one out by herself and we would have the other.

This car was a Studebaker Commander and was to be mine and Lorena's. It was a victoria with jump seats set behind the front seat and a back seat behind them. It had a storage compartment along one side which was covered with black velvet and specially built heavy bumpers both front and back. Why they were specially built or why we had them put on, I don't know, and I wouldn't remember them at all except for something that happened later. The tire cover on the back had a picture of a diving horse painted on it with the words: "The Great Carver Show—High-Diving Horses."

When we finally set out from California it was almost the first of the year, and we drove caravan style all the way from Sacramento to Pennsylvania, Al following us. It was beyond a doubt the best trip I had ever made; we could take our time and stop where we chose and not be hurried by train schedules. Although I was beginning my fifth year with the show, I still had not lost my hunger for travel. I enjoyed that journey with an intensity that still enables me to recall a time or place or person with amazing clarity. Only one mishap occurred.

On the second day out of Sacramento Lorena was driving (we took turns), when suddenly, for no apparent reason, she lost control and the car wheeled off to one side. By its own momentum it careened up onto a ridge, where it came to a sudden and violent halt and then teetered back and forth. The extra-heavy bumpers weighed it first down, then up, then down like a child's seesaw.

With the force of the stop the car suddenly seemed full of Pekinese. Candy and luggage and crackers shot forward in a flying mess. I can remember clearly that when the car finally stopped teetering Lorena reached up and adjusted the rear-view mirror.

We took stock and found that I had banged my knees and ruined my stockings but had suffered no other damage. Lorena had taken a punch in the stomach when she was thrown against the steering wheel. As we were sitting there sorting ourselves out from the crackers and candy, Al came around the bend in the Big 6 Special and slammed on the brakes. Jumping out, he ran over to us and stuck his head in the window. "What in the God damn hell," he said, "are you doing here?" There was never an adequate answer.

We reached Lorena's farm about the middle of January, and a few days later the horses arrived. There were now only three of them. Lightning had died and Judas had been traded after Dr. Carver's death for a horse named Apollo. We hated to lose Judas, but he had been useless ever since 1924, when he had been retired because of his too dangerous style of diving. Now that Dr. Carver was gone Al had forced himself to make the trade, since we needed a new horse desperately. John would be going out with Lorena, which would leave us only Klatawah, who was getting old. We knew we would have to retire him soon since he was nearly thirty, though he still worked with almost his usual fire. Daddy Carver had used Silver King and a horse named Powder Face until they were thirty-seven and thirty-eight years old, respectively, but they hadn't carried a rider, and it was harder on a horse in every way to have extra weight on his back. So we knew we must begin to look for a horse to take Klatawah's place, and Apollo was Al's choice.

Choices are never easy. With horses there is absolutely no way of knowing whether a likely-looking one will make a diver until you start to train him. The fact that a horse will jump in a river and swim across for his own pleasure when he is back on the farm does not mean that he will show the slightest inclination to jump off a forty-foot tower with a rider on his back. In fact, the odds are very much against it. This means that a lot of money and time and patience are usually expended before a new diver is found. Still, time and patience and money had to be spent if the act was to stay in business, so before leaving California, Al found Apollo and hoped he would work out.

At least he had the primary requisites. First of all, he was pretty. In the beginning he had been so painfully thin that his hipbones stuck out, but Al, with his eye for horseflesh, recognized his potential and by feeding him the best of everything turned the big rawboned buckskin with black mane and tail into a rather swanky-looking horse.

Second, he was a cold-blood, another of the requisites. Klatawah was our only thoroughbred horse, because as a rule thoroughbreds proved too temperamental. In an act such as ours the rider had to be certain an animal could be depended on to react in the same way time after time after time, and this was not usually true of thoroughbreds. They were so high-spirited that one could never be certain what they would do. The term "cold-blood" refers to any horse which is not a thoroughbred or a standard-bred (those bred for harness racing). An ordinary plow horse or farm horse is a cold-blood, and this is what Dr. Carver and Al always looked for.

Third, Apollo was young. He was about six years old, the right age to begin training. Younger than that, horses still feel coltish and behave accordingly. By the time they are six or seven, horses have worked most of the play out of their systems.

Finally, Apollo was a gelding. Dr. Carver always preferred stallions to mares and geldings to stallions because they were easier to handle. In the beginning he had tried to avoid having them castrated, so that they could be used later for breeding purposes, but Klatawah soon showed him that wouldn't do. Once when he was on the high tower, about to make a dive, a mare in season trotted up out front pulling a buggy, and Klatawah nearly tore down the tower getting to her. He backed down the long ramp, scraping the rider as he went. Dr. Carver decided not to risk a repetition of that performance. Always afterward when he bought a stallion he had him cut.

With the mares it was different. They did not become violent during the mating season, but they did get restless, and since there wasn't much a person could do but see them through it, Dr. Carver preferred not having them in the first place. Lightning and Snow had been the exceptions, but

Snow didn't carry a rider and was so temperamental anyway that it would have been hard to tell when she was in season and when she wasn't. Lightning's defense was that she was so beautiful no one could have resisted her no matter how much they might have wished to.

Even with these favorable characteristics, however, Apollo was an unknown quantity. Was he shy? Was he stubborn? Was he loyal? Was he brave?

No one knew and no one would know until we had begun his training. Horses are like people; they form likes and dislikes, experience anger, sorrow, joy, and loneliness, as well as cowardice and courage; and courage, the most important quality of all in a diving horse, cannot be taught. A person cannot whip a horse to courage any more than he can whip the fear out of him. In fact, whipping only increases the fear. Dr. Carver never owned a whip himself and never allowed his grooms to use one. "A whip-trained horse is a broken horse," he always said. "Our horses aren't whip-trained. Our horses are educated."

Al began Apollo's training in California and found his progress slow but felt that, once we were situated where we could go into intensive training, he would quickly improve. On the contrary, by the time a practice tower was put up and a tank dug on Lorena's farm, Apollo seemed to have forgotten everything he had learned. This was very strange, since experience had shown that a horse never retrogressed. Nevertheless, Apollo had retrogressed completely, and Al, to his supreme disgust, had to begin training from scratch.

Training is a lengthy process, taking weeks and sometimes months, during which a horse progresses from the low tower to the high just as a rider does. In the beginning a lead rope is put on the horse, attached to his diving harness and long enough to reach out to the front of the tank. Here the trainer takes his position, coaxing the horse to come off the twelve-foot tower and dive into the tank. This he does by tugging gently and constantly urging in a calm, sure voice. Sometimes a horse simply refuses to be budged by the tugs or the voice, and if he continues to do so over a reasonable length of time all efforts are abandoned and he is sold.

Usually, however, most animals can be talked into trying it at least once, and this was true of Apollo.' Al soon had him to the point where he would come off the low tower, but from the very first he showed an appalling lack of style. This was bad, for if a horse didn't have style he just didn't have it and, like courage, style is impossible to teach. In Apollo's case he came off the tower with all four feet spread as if he were trying to fly and invariably landed with a belly flop that sent water in all directions. He was awkward and ungainly by any standards, but Al kept working with him, hoping he would improve.

In the meantime he kept the lead rope on him, as he did with all the horses, even after they had graduated to the high tower, in order to help them get their heads up out of the water and keep them from strangling. It also helped guide them out of the tank. After a while, of course, a horse learned to take care of these details for himself, even to keeping the water out of his nose by sucking in his nostrils, as I had noticed Lightning do the first night I watched her dive.

Of course it was from the high tower that a horse really showed his spunk. From that height only the truly brave would dive and, as we were finding out more surely day by day, Apollo wasn't one of them. It soon became apparent that he was a dud.

The situation was actually very acute, since Al had signed more than the usual number of contracts for the coming season in the belief that by summer Apollo would be diving in form. Now in place of the mediocrity for which we would gladly have settled we had nothing at all.

About this time another problem arose to complicate matters further. Although the doctors had given Lorena permission to ride and she had ridden for Al the past two seasons, she decided, after thinking it over, that it would be too great a strain for her to ride as well as manage the act. She would be completely alone except for a groom to see to the horse and would have no help with the supervision of the tanks and building of the towers or with the financial side of things, so she decided she would get someone to dive for her. This would be easier than trying to find someone to manage the act, for it took years to learn the business. This meant that we now had the problem of finding a rider, which could be almost as difficult as finding a horse. In this instance, however, Fate took a hand and was kind. About the time Lorena decided to act as manager instead of performer, I had a letter from my sister Arnette.

Arnette was now fifteen years old. I was nine years older than she but more devoted to her than to the others because by the time she came along I was old enough to appreciate her. From the first there had been a bond between us and a closeness we were to continue to share for the rest of our lives.

She had been an admirer of mine since she was very small, and I had no sooner become a rider of diving horses than she wanted to learn to ride too. Of course she was much too young at the time and I had ignored her pleas, but now she was a junior in high school and I no longer had an excuse. She could join us for the summer and still be back in time to enroll for her senior year. As for her qualifications, from the pictures she had sent me I could see that, physically at least, she seemed ideally suited for the job.

Arnette was not as tall as I and somewhat heavier, but the heaviness was muscle, not fat. She also had a freshness about her that was very appealing. There was a radiance that struck everyone and prompted a friend of Mother's to refer to her as "the beauty of the family." I took the letter to Al, hoping he would agree to let her come. He said if I was willing it was all right with him.

Now all I had to do was decide whether I could afford to let her take the chances I knew a rider must take.

Ninety-five per cent of the time a horse's dives are good, and if a rider has the proper training she can take care of the other five per cent; but there are accidents in everything, and they are more likely to happen to people who put themselves in dangerous positions than they are to those who do not. By allowing my little sister to come I would certainly be placing her in greater jeopardy than if she stayed at home.

On the other hand, Arnette resembled me. She didn't want life to be ordinary; she craved experience as I did and I wasn't certain that by refusing to let her come I'd be doing her any favor. After all, the most and worst that had ever happened to me were friction burns on my legs, a sprained ankle once when Klatawah took off at an angle and twisted my foot between himself and the uprights, and a bang on the head I received one night when he turned over with me still on him and I hit the bottom of the tank. Still, there were girls who had been injured more seriously.

One had had her front teeth knocked out and another had broken her nose. Another had fractured a cheekbone, which left a sunken place in her cheek. Worst of all, one man had actually been killed. Though it was true he had not been a member of the troupe, he had been a Hollywood stunt man and should have known how to handle himself. He begged Dr. Carver to let him ride so that he could have some publicity pictures made, and Dr. Carver finally agreed. He went in all right but he didn't come up, and when rescuers dived in and dragged him out they found he had broken his neck.

In spite of all the negative arguments, however, I felt that if Arnette had any real talent for riding I could teach her, and if I taught her as carefully as Dr. Carver had taught me she'd be safe.

Having settled the mental debate to my satisfaction, I sat down and wrote her to come, and almost immediately got a reply saying that the school was going to let her take her exams early that year and that she would arrive sometime about the middle of May. May 15 was a month before Lorena's season opened, which allowed enough time for training. Many girls learned to ride quickly, more quickly than I had. If she was in as excellent physical condition as she appeared to be in her pictures, I might be able to dispense with her ground training and start her off on the low platform.

On the day Arnette arrived Al and I met her at the station. The first thing I noticed was that she had cut her hair. "Arnette," I said darkly, "I wrote you not to cut it. We like our riders to look like girls, not like boys. You look perfectly terrible."

But beyond a meaningful look which said more than words, she ignored the remark. I realized then that Arnette had been old enough to remember full well the time I had cut my own hair, and in view of the fact that I could recall clearly how it had looked lying on Mamie Lou's floor, I could not very well go on scolding her. Besides, I was glad to see her.

I kept her on ground training only a week because she was, as I had hoped, in excellent physical condition. Nevertheless, I was far more nervous than she when I sent her up to the low tower to make her first dive. She proved to me quickly, however, that I needn't have worried. She came off like a pro and stayed with the horse all the way. We both knew that the real test was still ahead of her but were very encouraged. She continued to make such excellent practice dives that I could not shrug off her pleas when she began to beg to go off the high tower a week later.

Time was creeping up on us, and the sooner I got her up there, the better, but even more persuasive was the memory of my own pleas and how they had been ignored. The week of waiting before making my first dive from the high tower had been a cruel and brutal one and I was determined to spare her that if I could. Therefore, in spite of a warning voice that told me not to rush things, I decided to let her try.

The next morning when she got up on the tower I was literally holding my breath, but, to my great joy and the complete fulfillment of all my expectations, she made a perfect dive. Al and I were both jubilant, and so was Lorena.

We had no sooner begun to congratulate one another, however, than things began to go wrong. One time Arnette's timing would be off, another time she would lose control of the horse. I realized too late that I had done her an injustice by letting her cut short her training, for lack of technique can be serious. Danger is always increased when a rider is too inexperienced to analyze her faults and figure out how to correct them. Also, a horse is accustomed to having someone on his back who knows what she's doing, and an unskilled rider can ruin a well-trained horse very quickly. But there was no turning back.

I was diverted from my concern over my sister by our discouragement with Apollo. By now fair time was almost upon us and we had no horse but Klatawah. We couldn't possibly expect him to make two or three dives a day seven days a week; he had to have some relief. All we could do was cancel some of our contracts.

Al didn't like this, but his back was to the wall. He wrote to three of his commitments saying we couldn't come. Instead of replying by return mail, all three fair managers promptly appeared on Lorena's doorstep. "We've been counting on you as our big drawing card," each said. "There's not time to get anyone else. We've advertised the act. You've got to come. You can't back out."

Al tried to make them understand the situation, but all three remained adamant. There was nothing to do but agree to fulfill the contracts, which, as Al said later, was the most foolish promise he had ever made in his life. How could he possibly find and train a horse in the space of a few weeks? It always took months. Ridiculous though the search seemed, he had to try. Each morning he filled up the gas tank of the car and drove around the countryside. Within a radius of many miles he looked in every field and pasture for a potential diving horse—a pretty horse, an intelligent horse, a horse that would prove to have courage and pride—and the days passed, and still Al found no horse. Then one day when he was on his way home after another fruitless exploration, he came up over a hill and rolled along beside a pasture, and there, standing apart from a group of horses, was a beautiful paint.

He slammed on the brakes, got out of the car, and walked closer. The paint turned and stared with frosty blue eyes and then kicked up his heels and ran off. Al went back to his car and followed a road that led to a farmhouse in the distance. A man was standing on the porch.

"My name's Al Carver," Al said. "I want to buy that paint."

"Glad to know you, Mr. Carver. You're not the first one."

"What will it take to buy him?"

"Wouldn't sell him to my worst enemy."

"What do you mean, you wouldn't sell him to your worst enemy?"

"I mean the fellow's an outlaw. You can't ride him, you can't put him to the plow, you can't even be nice to him. Little bit more, I tell you, and that horse would be a killer."

"I still want him," said Al. "How much will he cost?"

"Sold him three times already. Folks always bring him back."

"I won't bring him back," promised Al. "Come on now. How much?"

"Been using him as a kind of decoy. Put him out there in the pasture. Folks stop to look at him and I end up selling them one of the others."

"I can't use any of the others," Al said. "I've got to have that one."

As Al told us, the argument went on and on, and finally the man agreed to sell the outlaw, but Al had to promise to bring him back if he didn't work out. "You understand how it is," the farmer said. "I don't like to lose my decoy."

That afternoon I heard Al's car coming and could tell by the sound of it that it was pulling a loaded trailer. I dashed out to the entrance gate just as he pulled in.

"Oh, Al," I exclaimed, "he's beautiful!"

"Yeah," Al said.

"What do you mean, yeah'? You don't sound too happy."

"I'm a little skittish about him. The man I bought him from says he's an outlaw."

"Outlaw?" I looked at the horse incredulously. He didn't look like an outlaw to me.

The groom let him down out of the trailer, and our new horse looked around with the curiosity most animals show in a strange location.

He was, I saw, a stockily built white horse with bay markings, blue eyes, and a black tail. He was beautiful and sleek and, though obviously spirited, did not look like a villain. I walked up to him and patted him on the neck, speaking to him soothingly at the same time, and was pleased when he nudged me gently as if to confirm my belief in him. Then he suddenly caught hold of a ruffle at the neck of my dress and tore the dress off me!

For a moment I stood there in my slip, shocked to my bones. He hadn't been nudging me out of friendship but in order to get hold of the ruffle! I turned and ran toward the house, feeling a terrible fool.

From such a beginning it might have been expected that Red Lips (as Al's discovery was named) and I would have our troubles, but the fact was that as time went by I came to love him as I loved no other animal. I discovered that his tearing my dress off had not been done out of animosity. He simply liked to tear things by pulling them to pieces with his teeth. If the groom wasn't careful to remove his blanket after drying him, he would pull it off his back and, holding it down with his front feet, rip it to shreds. But that was only a minor idiosyncrasy. He was so beautiful and so vital that I got a thrill out of just watching him, and it wasn't long before I began to refer to him as "mine."

Ten

The new horse showed his true colors on the following morning when Al began his training. Contrary to what we had expected, he did not display the slightest resentment toward the halter or lead rope when they were put on him. What was more, he went up the ramp to the low platform as if he had been doing it all his life. When he got to the front he stood there for a moment and then, with only the suggestion of a pull on the rope from Al, slid his feet down on the kickoff board and dived.

Very possibly there have never been two more astonished people in the world. Then, in mortal fear that the first dive was a fluke, Al sent him up again. But again he came off as smoothly as a veteran. Furthermore, he had style, grace, fire, and form and worked with the greatest enthusiasm. Within a few weeks' time he was doing as well as horses that had been diving for months.

Ordinarily it takes about two years to train a horse fully. I do not mean that a horse cannot be diving from the forty-foot tower before that time, but it usually takes that long for him to become a consistently good performer in his particular style. Some horses are never successful, even though they have plenty of nerve, because they can't get the knack of the take-off. Others seem unable to control their leg movements while in the air, and still others prove to be poor swimmers. (The latter begin to stroke with their forelegs only when they start up from the bottom of the tank, letting their back legs drag as weights. They usually try to overcome this error by stroking harder with their forefeet and, as a consequence, bring themselves up too high out of the water, lose their balance, and roll over.)

Happily, Red had none of these faults. He was not only a graceful diver but a good swimmer and quickly became so proficient that we decided we could put a rider on him well ahead of the customary period in a horse's training. Thus his training could be speeded up; we would not only be teaching him to dive but to carry a rider as well.

To understand what this meant in relation to Red, it must be remembered that he reportedly had never allowed anyone on his back. We hadn't the least idea what kind of fit he might throw when I mounted, and Al told me beforehand that if he showed any signs of misbehaving I should get off immediately and let him dive alone. But aside from one frosty look, everything went smoothly. I patted Red on the neck and talked to him in a quiet, reassuring voice, and after a few minutes he went over to the edge of the tower and dived.

From then on I went out every morning and rode him in his training dives until it was time for us to leave for the fairs, the first of which was in upstate New York. There I worked him every morning and also rode him during the afternoon performance to accustom him to the crowd. He continued to behave beautifully from the low tower. We were sufficiently encouraged for Al to instruct our advance man (who went on ahead to supervise the building of the towers at the next three fairs we were to work) to cut down slightly on the height of the tower because we intended to try Red from the top as soon as possible.

When the New York fair closed we left for Canada, and the morning of the opening day we went out to the grounds to practice. I was to have my first ride on Red from the high tower and admittedly was nervous.

After I got up on the tower Al turned him into the runway and he came trotting up the ramp as though he had done it thousands of times. He allowed me to mount him all right and brought up at the head of the platform properly, but he was a little slow in the take-off and, for some unexplained reason, just before he left the board the harness started slipping. I lost my position as he kicked off, and somewhere about mid-air my body lost contact with his. I remained connected to him only by means of my grip on the diving harness, and I lost even that when we hit. He went in on his right shoulder and we came up on opposite sides of the tank. By putting some extra pep into my stroke I managed to swim over and climb on again before he reached the incline.

It was a point of the greatest pride with me that when I did get knocked off I got back on as quickly as possible. I felt it was the only way I could redeem myself.

When we came out of the tank Al said he thought I should let Red try it alone. That way the horse could get used to the height by himself, and it would give me an opportunity to study his action and style.

This time he worked with more speed, but it sent shivers down my spine, for instead of making a plunge dive he went in on his nose! A nose diver is the most difficult of all to ride, and I knew that if Red dived that straight with me on his back and I didn't turn him over I'd be better than I thought I was. John had thrown in a nose dive now and then, but he was big and powerful enough to handle a rider's weight with ease; also, he was an accomplished diver who knew how to throw his long neck and head up to balance himself.

That day, the hours until performance time seemed to last forever, but my anxiety was needless. When the time came Red went off like a trouper in a perfect medium plunge. From then on he improved. Some of his dives were bad, of course, but most of them were good. During the last of those memorable three weeks, however, he managed to give me one really big scare.

At a fair in St. John, New Brunswick, the soil was so gravelly that we had had to shore up the sides of the tank. On returning from dinner one evening we found that the posts on the left side had washed loose and the canvas on the left wall was caving in and floating up from the bottom. It was not bad enough to cause damage, provided the horse landed in the exact center of the tank, but unfortunately Red had developed a marked tendency to veer to the left. If he did so that night he would dive directly into the posts and the results would surely be deadly.

Normally in such circumstances we would have gone to the secretary of the fair and explained that we would be unable to give the performance. Our contract covered the possibility of dangerous situations and gave us the right to cancel performances, but in St. John that summer other considerations made cancellation inadvisable.

Some of the acts had not been able to appear at the fair until the middle of the week because of some immigration trouble at the Canadian border. Their tardy appearance, coupled with heavy mists which kept the stage and props so wet that it was hard for the performers to accomplish their tricks properly, had created a feeling of dissatisfaction among the members of the fair association, and there were rumors that these acts would not receive their money. If this were true we felt that our refusal to dive the horse would further jeopardize their position—and perhaps our own.

A grandstand that gradually filled to capacity that night was further proof that we had to devise some means of diving the horse. To put the wall back where it belonged was impossible. We would have had to pump all the water out and then take the canvas out, and there just wasn't time for all that. Finally I came up with a suggestion.

If we took the long rope used for exercising the horses up to top the tower before performance time and threw one end down to the ground on the right side of the tank, I could snap the other end onto Red Lips' halter before I mounted him and Al could guide his dive to the right. By pulling in that direction as we came off the tower he could keep the horse from veering left into the piling. It wasn't a foolproof solution, but it was better than nothing, so we decided to try it.

All went well until I snapped the rope onto his halter, signaled for the slack to be taken up, and mounted. Unfortunately, however, the slack wasn't taken up quickly enough and the horse stepped neatly into a coil of rope on the floor of the tower. I became upset, knowing that Red was very fussy about his feet; this irritant at a crucial moment might well put him off his stride. Alternatively, I had visions of him diving with his feet all tangled in the rope, making him incapable of swimming up from the bottom.

Greatly excited, I called down to Al and explained what had happened. "Release the rope if you can reach the snap," he shouted, and I leaned as far forward as possible and managed to reach and unsnap it. This was something new to Red, and the delay made him nervous. I was hardly back into riding position when he started to dive. As we took off I breathed a fervent prayer: "O God, please make this horse dive straight." I do not know whether God had time to hear me, but Red landed in the center of the tank.

As time went on that season Red became more and more fond of nose diving and, before it was over, had dumped me several times. I also turned him over on three different occasions, but past experience helped me save myself from any serious injury. Later I learned to duck at precisely the right moment and thereafter seldom lost him.

Although Al and I became increasingly devoted to Red, it was easy for us to understand why his former owner had branded him an outlaw. He was as obstinate as any mule that ever lived. The only way to cope with him was to outsmart him, and that was quite a task because he was extremely intelligent. One thing became obvious—using force was never going to make Red do anything he didn't want to do. The moment he suspected he was being forced he would get ready for battle.

He first demonstrated this characteristic when I tried to ride him in a parade. (We didn't do that kind of thing as a rule, but arrangements had been made for all the performers to parade before the grandstand on the first night.) To my great surprise, when I got on his back he simply balked. He didn't buck like a bronco; instead he reared and tried to throw himself backward. He wasn't successful in tossing me, but it was obvious that he would keep on trying until he did or until he hurt himself. I had to get off—temporarily. We felt it would be bad for Red to think he could have his own way by a little extracurricular bucking, so we compromised and the groom led us through the parade. By pulling down hard on the halter he was able to make Red keep all four feet on the ground.

Red was a temperamental horse but worth the trouble entailed in humoring him. One day near the end of the season Al bought him a goat. (For reasons known only to horses, goats have a soothing effect upon them.) When I first met Happy, the goat was so little he fit into Al's hand, and I could not believe anything bite-sized could have any influence on Red. I followed Al out to see how the horse would take to his new companion.

Al walked into Red's stall, still holding the goat, and said, "All right, Red, this is your roommate. His name is Happy and he's a baby goat and you've got to be nice to him. See how little he is?" He held him up to Red, and Red took one look and rolled his eyes.

"Come on now," Al said, "you mustn't hurt him. He's too little to hurt. Come on and tell him hello. Make him feel at home." As he continued to chatter, he was making Happy a nest in the hay, and when he finished he put Happy in it and beckoned to the horse. Red, still looking wary, went over and nuzzled the tiny goat.

Happy let out a sad little bleat, and Red drew back quickly. Then, apparently having decided the bleat didn't mean much, Red snuffled him again. This time Happy did not bleat but began to look sleepy.

"That's the boy," soothed Al. "Make him feel at home." After a few minutes of walking around him and looking him over Red lay down beside the goat and the two of them went to sleep. From that moment on Happy slept with Red and Red looked out for him. He never rolled over on him or stepped on him or harmed him in any way.

As Happy grew bigger he began to wander away from the stall during the day and found that his mere presence outside the barn was sufficient to set the stable dogs barking. At first this frightened him half to death and he would run for Red's stall lickety-brindle. There he would place himself between Red's front legs, where he knew the dogs wouldn't dare to come after him.

This worked out so well that it turned into a game. Having learned that Red Lips was his protector, he began to bait the dogs deliberately. He would drift toward the front of the barn and out into the open just long enough to be seen, then light out for Red's stall and take his stand between the horse's feet. He would duck his head menacingly and paw the ground a little as if to show the dog and Red how fierce he was, but he never ventured from beneath the protection of his Colossus.

Later, however, Happy grew a formidable set of horns, and then the ground rules changed. He would go out long enough to attract the dogs, then run as usual for the stall, but, just short of it, he would wheel suddenly and meet the dog head on. Inevitably the dogs would go off howling; after each fracas Happy would turn to Red Lips with a look that seemed to say, "See, I'm a big goat now. I can take care of myself."

Happy's increasing size became a problem, not to us, but to Red, who solved it in his own intelligent way. In the beginning Happy had formed the habit of lying down in the hay to eat. This hadn't bothered Red because Happy was so small that he didn't take up much room, but when Happy got bigger the limited floor space presented difficulties. Happy still insisted on lying down in the middle of the hay to eat, and if Red wanted a meal he had to eat around him. Finally this got to be too much for Red, and one day we heard a mournful bleating from the barn. Al and I both went to see what was going on and found Happy running around soaking wet.

We could not imagine how it had happened since there was no puddle anywhere, but then, as if to demonstrate, Happy lay down in the middle of the hay and began to eat, whereupon Red turned and went to his water bucket, filled his mouth with water, and spat it out all over the goat. It was an imaginative solution to a domestic crisis.

Eleven

September came finally, and with it Lorena and Arnette. Lorena told me that although Arnette had come through the season unscathed there had been times when she wished she didn't have to watch her ride. She never knew whether Arnette was going to be skilled or whether she was going to be dangerously awkward. In spite of all attempts to correct her errors, Arnette continued to dive erratically. We agreed then that, although Arnette loved riding the diving horses, for some reason she wasn't a performer. I made up my mind then and there that no matter how hard Arnette pleaded she had ridden her last.

When I broke the verdict to Arnette she wailed just as I suspected she would, but I put her on the train and said, "Now go home and graduate cum laude and forget about this riding." As the train pulled out and disappeared from sight, I heaved a long sigh of relief.

By that time Al and I had been working together for a year, traveling all over the country, hardly out of one another's sight for more than a few hours. Al was some twenty years older than I and I had not thought him my "type," but as the months passed I had come to know him much better.

We talked about everything. We entertained each other for hours with stories of our childhoods and endlessly discussed the horses and the problems associated with them. I could share all his concerns about the act and he could understand my feelings. I suppose we both should have known that the inevitable was happening.

Al says he loved me from the beginning and that he had told himself soon after we met, "Someday I'm going to marry her," which is very flattering but from my viewpoint open to argument. Beyond a casual courtesy, he never evidenced any interest in me, at least not during his father's lifetime. But I suppose that's the clue. Al knew any attentions to me would meet with strong disapproval because Dr. Carver didn't make any bones about the fact that he thought his son "wild." Now that Dr. Carver was gone, however, Al could display his feelings, but, with a showman's true sense of timing, waited until I could know him better.

The first hint I had came from his eyes. They were deeply expressive, and a look appeared that I seemed to recognize but could not fully interpret. Whatever its meaning, it left me breathless and full of anticipation. It was like waking on a spring morning and listening to things come alive and knowing, even before you opened your eyes, that this day was going to be different. Until one night when we were making our last fair appearance in Connecticut, we never discussed being in love.

Driving back to the hotel that night, Al pulled my head down on his shoulder and quietly told me he loved me. In order to understand my reaction to this, I must make it clear that I had long since made up my mind never to marry— a decision compounded of several factors, the strongest of which was early conditioning. I had felt the conflicts in my parents' marriage and wanted no more of such misery. Too, from what I had seen of married couples in general, it appeared that, after the bloom of the honeymoon wore off, indifference always resulted—an emotion so pale and unpalatable that downright hatred is preferable. There was also a widespread social condition that prevailed during my childhood in the South that caused me to feel as I did. Families were much larger than most people could afford; they provided a financial quicksand in which parents struggled hopelessly all their lives.

I stammered out these anti-matrimonial views in one form or another that night, but, for all the good it did me, I might as well have saved my breath. Al was as strong-willed and strong-minded as his father, and when I finished all he said was, "That's silly."

"It's not silly," I said. "I'm serious."

"That's because you're young."

"I'm twenty-five!"

"That's young," he said. He was quiet a minute, then said, "I told you I loved you."

"I know," I said.

"And you love me," he said positively.

"I do?" I said.

In the days that followed, Al bent all my arguments from swords into plowshares, and one October evening I gave in and said that I would marry him.

The next morning I put on my brown chiffon dress and brown suede shoes and brown felt hat but still could not really believe I was getting married. It was as if someone had wound me up and pointed me in a certain direction and that's the way I was going.

We went to the little New England town of Norwich and found the justice of the peace, and in what seemed an incredibly short period of time I found myself standing beside Al, saying faintly, "I do," in the meantime being not at all certain I did. Afterward we drove back to the fairgrounds for my afternoon appearance, and when Al got out of the car and went over to the barn to check with the groom about the horses I watched him walk away from me, thinking, "I'm his wife!"

In a moment he came back and stood by the car door. Looking in at me, he said, "I'll see to it that you're never sorry." Then he leaned in the window and kissed me.

"People don't know we're married," I said.

He smiled. "They will."

The week after we were married Al brought me a present. It wasn't the kind of present many new brides would have appreciated or made use of, but it was the perfect one for me: a contract for a season's engagement at the Atlantic City Steel Pier.

Atlantic City at that time was the queen of the amusement-park business, and the biggest names in show business appeared there during the summer.

Our contract at the Steel Pier was by far the most lucrative one the Carver act had ever achieved, and when Al signed it I was more excited than I had ever been in my life. I knew that this would be the high spot of my riding career and I was anxious for the winter to pass and spring to come so we could get started.

After we had mailed the signed contract the management of the pier wrote, saying they wanted the horses to dive into the ocean, but with the memory of Lightning's death still so vivid in our minds we refused. The management replied, "Never mind. We want your act. We'll build anything you need." Early that spring we went to Atlantic City to see to the tower and tank.

Until then the pier had ended in a ballroom with a wide deck running around it, but our arrival produced drastic changes. A grandstand, large enough to seat eight thousand spectators, rose from the floor of the deck to up under the eaves of the ballroom. Since I would be riding three times a day on weekdays and four times a day on weekends until the middle of July, after which I'd do four, five, or six shows a day through September, by the end of the season I would have performed before a tremendous number of people.

After the grandstand was finished they began on the stage, which was to stand sixty feet beyond the grandstand and twenty-five feet above the water at high tide. It had to be connected to the deck by means of a narrow cross bridge for the use of the performers.

Next the ramp of our diving tower was built across the back of the stage so as to give the spectators a broadside view. The tank was then cut into the floor of the stage and supported by hundreds of pilings. Five feet of it rose above the stage and six feet sank below. To allow for the five feet above the deck, we raised the height of the diving platform from forty to forty-five feet.

I had a dressing room to myself which adjoined one belonging to Al It was not large—only about six feet square-but had everything in it I needed. A long shelf ran along one wall for my make-up and odds and ends, and from a window over the shelf I could see out by standing on my toes. I kept my wardrobe trunks containing all my suits and other paraphernalia in a corner and had hooks on the opposite wall for my wet suits.

Al's room was slightly larger than mine and we made it into a small lounge. It contained a rocking chair, along one wall a bench covered with a leather cushion, and his trunks. This was where I was to spend the better part of my time between acts, either reading or talking with other performers who dropped in to chat.

To the back of the stage and our tower a high wall was built which screened off-duty performers from the eyes of the audience. It was the equivalent of Broadway's "greenroom," and here they took sun baths, read, did fancywork, practiced their tricks, gossiped or gambled. Poker and crap shooting were the most popular games with the men, since a player could leave without breaking up the game.

The horses were quartered in special stalls that faced a wide corridor toward the front of the pier. Here people passing on their way to the grandstand were able to see them. The horses were protected by walls of glass so that no one could feed or tease them, and our groom was quartered there both day and night. When a horse was ready for his act, he was led from his stall along the pier to the rear of the stage, from where he mounted the ramp.

I was tremendously pleased with the arrangements and wrote a detailed report to Arnette. She replied at once, saying that she knew I wouldn't let her ride but couldn't she come and stay with us that summer and find something else to do on the pier? This appeal was irresistible and I wrote her to come. I then made some arrangements for her to see the manager of a water-sports act consisting of swimming and diving and riding on water skis. Arnette had never done any water skiing, but I felt confident that it wouldn't take her long to learn.

After the manager interviewed her and watched her swim and dive he agreed she would do as one of the two girls in the act. Thus there began a series of summers at Atlantic City—1929,1930,1931, and 1932.

Twelve

The first year at the pier there were only a few regular acts: the diving horses, a human cannon ball who was shot into the ocean instead of a net, a troupe of Hawaiian divers, an aerial-ladder act, and the water-sports gang. We had special acts on weekends which included some big-name bands, and a trio of musical clowns appeared for a couple of weeks, but the show was largely unpretentious. The following year Mr. Endicott, the manager, decided to go all out and get big names. He proceeded to sign up famous performers.

Johnny Weissmuller, who won the gold medal for freestyle swimming at the 1928 Olympics, was at that time moving from amateur to pro and putting on swimming exhibitions across the country. He was signed up for six weeks at the pier. Eddie Cantor and George Jessel were to come down from New York on successive weekends, and in the band category Paul Whiteman and John Philip Sousa (who had appeared one weekend during the previous season) were scheduled.

Sousa and his band had been so popular that Mr. Endicott booked him for several weeks running this time, in the course of which he and Al became good friends. He was a genial old fellow who loved to spend his time backstage talking with the performers, and he often told stories about the old days to which we listened eagerly. Although he must have been about seventy by that time, he was lively as a cricket and had snow-white hair and white mustaches and always wore a snappy white cap with his bemedaled navy-blue uniform. He directed the band with a quick flick of the wrist which miraculously seemed sufficient to co-ordinate the whole enormous band. His famous marches filled the air every afternoon and evening to the delight of enthusiastic audiences.

In addition to the celebrities, the program contained a number of acts with names less widely known but considered by people in show business to be tops. Some of these had joined us from circuses, to which they returned after their Atlantic City engagements were finished. One of the best was Oscar Babcock and his loop-the-loop bicycle act, and another was "The Globe of Death." Both acts were gravity-defying stunts, the latter being one in which a man and his wife rode motorcycles round and round inside their globe until they worked up sufficient momentum to carry them up over the top. Oscar put his bicycle through a metal figure eight with a wide gap in it at one point so that for a moment he was not only defying gravity but actually flying free.

There was also a comedy routine based on the comic strip "Barney Google" in which two men, Douglas Wright (better known as "Sparkey") and Kelsey, his partner, did a clown act inside a big baggy cotton horse made up to look like Spark Plug, even to the enormous feet and patched blanket. Among other things, they did a zany bandy-legged waltz which always brought shouts of laughter.

Several animal acts, notably the Pallenberg bears, appeared during the summer. Mr. Pallenberg trained the bears and Mrs. Pallenberg put them through their paces. They juggled and danced and, as a finale, got into boats and rowed around in our tank.

Three holdovers from the previous season, who were to become a hard core of veterans at the Steel Pier, completed the roster: the diving horses, the Hawaiians (four men and a woman who dived from a 105-foot tower), and the water-sports gang (five men and two women). An aerial act, made up in part from the troupe which had been there the year before, was also on the bill. It was called "The Fearless Falcons," namely Irene Berger and Orville and Roxie LaRose.

We met Orville and Roxie in 1928 while appearing at the Cotton Palace in Waco, Texas. At that time Roxie, a beautiful blue-eyed, fair-skinned, titian-haired woman, had been working alone atop a ninety-foot perch while Orville, dark, slight, but unusually strong for his size, had combined the duties of manager and rigging man. The contrast between them was not limited to their physical appearance. Roxie was a rather serious-minded person, whereas Orville was a natural clown. His humor was not really original, but his gift for remembering jokes and the timing of his wisecracks enabled him to make almost any situation amusing.

The year before we had encountered the third Falcon. Irene was then one of the "Four Verses," aerialists working on a two-ladder rigging 104 feet high. The first thing I noticed about her was a gorgeous pair of glistening, long-lashed brown eyes. She weighed about a hundred and twenty pounds but looked smaller because her flesh was compact. Her muscles were developed to such an extent that off stage she appeared slightly muscle-bound, but in the air, where she could bring her muscles into play, she proved to be the most exciting aerial performer I had ever watched.

After her first season at the Steel Pier, Irene left the Verses troupe and joined Orville and Roxie. The new act consisted of Roxie and Irene up on perch poles in what is termed a "double." Orville had spent the winter personally designing and building special rigging for the act. The rigging included two poles about five feet apart and about 125 feet high—the height of a twelve-story building—and they never worked with a net.

Both women were experts at their business, but Irene was more than expert; she was an artist. Watching her, I had the feeling that she had been only half alive on the ground and not until she reached the top of the rigging did she find her native element. Roxie was clever and graceful, but she moved about in the rigging as if well aware that death lurked in the background, not fearfully, but simply determined not to tempt fate too far. On the other hand, Irene worked with an abandon that seemed deliberate, taunting, as if she were figuratively thumbing her nose. As one member of the Bonelli troupe (a revolving ladder act brought over from Europe for a brief appearance) said, "When I watch Irene, she makes my heart fall down into my pants."

We began our 1931 season about the middle of May, just as in previous years, and the summer moved forward into July at its usual pace. When the night of July 14 came around it was like a hundred others. Crowds swarmed the boardwalk and spilled out onto the beach, and music drifted across the water from Steeplechase Pier, where lighted Ferris wheels spun giddy circles of light. Tired children dragged at their parents' hands, their faces sticky with cotton candy, and the smell of fresh sea air was wonderful as it came in off the water.

Walking along to my dressing room, I was vaguely aware of the Atlantic City boardwalk atmosphere the way a person is aware that an old and familiar song is playing in the background. There was nowhere any sense of impending disaster.

In my dressing room I went through the motions of putting on my bathing suit and draped a shawl over my shoulders. When I finished putting on my make-up I went outside to a bench near my door where I often sat in the evening to listen to the music. I was always conscious of the music because it provided my cue for getting ready to go on. As I listened to "Springtime in the Rockies" I knew that Roxie and Irene were reaching the climax of their act on the perch poles and would soon be coming down. Our act was the finale and always followed theirs.

Then I got up and walked over to where some of the other performers had congregated and spoke briefly to Tommy Kao, one of the Hawaiians. From where I stood I could see the front and rear ends of the horse costume Sparkey and Kelsey had just taken off and laid over a bench. A long-lashed eye looked up coyly at me.

In a moment Dempsey, the little fox terrier we had recently acquired, ran around the comer. He was barking fiercely, which meant that Red Lips was coming. Dempsey had taken it upon himself to escort Red Lips from the stalls up to the ramp, seeming to announce to everyone, "This is my horse! Get out of the way!"

George appeared with Red and led him to the bottom of the ramp, and as the music swung into "The Stars and Stripes Forever" I went over to them.

The Falcons always swung down on "The Stars and Stripes Forever," Roxie by means of an iron jaw (that is, by clamping her teeth tightly on a special grip at the end of a long rope paid out by men on the ground) and Irene in a arabesque above Roxie on the same rope, a position that resembles a swan dive and is very beautiful. There was a "Ta rah!" and I knew that they were down. A burst of applause followed as they made their bows, and when it became scattered I took off my shawl and laid it over the railing.

I tried to time my arrival at the top of the platform with Al's final words, for this was the most effective moment. I heard Al say, "Ladies and gentlemen, all eyes cast atop this lof-ty tower," and began to climb. Just as he said, "And so we present for your entertainment the most exciting act in show business today—Miss Sonora and Red Lips, the famous diving horse," I stepped onto the platform and the spots lit up behind me.

The audience burst into applause in the grandstand below and I waved to them. Then I seated myself on the railing and, when I was ready, signaled George to send Red up. Immediately he circled the horse and then sent him onto the runway at a gallop. The heavy drum of Red's hoofs vibrated on the ramp as he came up, and then he was dashing past me. Instantly I reached out and in a single motion grabbed the harness and slid across his back.

Red had a little dance he performed before he kicked off. He would lift first one foot and then the other, as if he couldn't make up his mind which one to use; then he would slide both feet over the edge of the platform and dive.

Tonight he went through his routine and the kickoff came as usual, but for some reason he seemed to go into an unusually straight-down nose dive. Normally I would have ducked just before hitting the water and would have entered the tank head foremost, but this time his body was in such an extremely perpendicular position that I was afraid of throwing him over on his back. Several times before on a nose dive I had struck the water in an upside-down position, a method of landing that can be both painful and dangerous, for even if the rider escapes without serious injury she gets a severe shaking up. I had to make a split-second decision, and in a desperate effort to avoid turning him over I stiffened my arms and held my weight back, hoping to maintain our balance. I was successful, but that position caused me to strike the water flat on my face instead of diving in on the top of my head. In the excitement of the moment I failed to close my eyes quickly enough, and as we hit I felt a dull stinging sensation. A second or two later, when the horse and I emerged from the water, I was still on his back. As I dismounted and reached for the sugar to reward Red, Al said, "That was a toughie, wasn't it?"

I said, "Yes, it was. I took it right in the eyes."

"Did it hurt?"

"Yes, it stung like the mischief for a minute, but I'm all right now," and as I turned to go to my dressing room I thought that I was.

I had almost finished taking off my wet suit and putting on a dry one in preparation for my second appearance that evening when my vision suddenly clouded. Patchy bits of white fog floated before my eyes. As I came out and closed the dressing-room door, Al, who was waiting for me, asked, "Are you sure you're all right?"

"Yes," I said, "but that dive gave me more of a slap in the eyes than I thought. I feel as if I were trying to peer through fog."

"In that case," he said, "you're going to a doctor."

"No, I'm not," I said. My personal experience with doctors had not been extensive, but I suspected that a favorite medical trick was to immobilize a patient, and no one was going to put me off my horse because of patches of fog. "I'm all right. Whatever's the matter, it can't be very serious because it doesn't hurt at all."

Although Al kept insisting, I rode again that night. I also rode the next day and the one following. I still saw pieces of fog, but aside from the momentary sting I had felt when I hit the water I had no pain whatsoever. I reassured myself with the theory that if a small cinder in the eye could cause intense pain, then any truly serious injury to my eyes would have been unbearable. This homemade diagnosis enabled me to continue riding with a clear conscience.

After several days the fogginess began to vanish but was supplanted by another condition which developed rapidly. I had the peculiar sensation that I was wearing a yellow eye-shade, but when I looked up in an effort to find out what caused the sensation, the effect disappeared. Since it went away so easily I decided it couldn't be very serious either and continued diving, not saying anything to anyone. Then on August 1, at the nine o'clock show, I had an extremely rough ride on Klatawah. Back in my dressing room, I became alarmed, because for the first time a smoky gray curtain blanked out all but the largest and brightest-colored objects in the room. I automatically changed into another suit, ready to make my second ride, and opened the door to get a breath of fresh air. Then I sat down and with my head on my arms faced up to some belated worrying. George, our groom, who had been drying and blanketing Klatawah just outside, noticed me sitting there and asked, "Is anything wrong, Miss Sonora?"

"I don't know," I said. "It was a tough ride but I didn't get hurt. Still, I can barely see anything at all. It's like looking through a thick screen of smoke."

I hadn't told Al that I had landed again on my face because I didn't want to worry him, but George took it upon himself to summon Al. Immediately he was at my door, full of concern and questions. In spite of his objections, I insisted on making another ride that night; he could summon no arguments strong enough to talk me out of it. By this time I was behaving under some insane compulsion that had nothing to do with common sense. "The show must go on," I told myself. "There's no one but me to ride," but in effect what I was doing was denying that anything was wrong. I was also protecting my pride. No one had ever had to take my place on my horse and no one was going to.

As Red Lips galloped up the ramp later that evening I thought to myself, "Thank God he's got a lot of white on him. I could never have seen Klatawah's dark coat against the night background."

After the last dive we went home and I went to bed. I refused to have any discussion of my eyes, still insisting that I was all right. The next morning brilliant sunshine penetrated the gray curtain and made it seem less sinister. I told Al and Arnette to go ahead to the pier, since they had to be there earlier than I did, and promised to come along later. Then I dressed, had my breakfast, and set forth.

I covered the four blocks from our apartment to the pier and there had a mishap, seemingly unimportant in itself, that frightened me more than anything that had happened so far. At the entrance I became confused and walked through the main gate instead of the one reserved for employees. I recognized my mistake almost immediately, for I heard people moving all around me and realized I was in a much more heavily populated place than our private walkway. What I had done thoroughly upset me; I knew that if I could get lost in such familiar surroundings I must hardly be able to see at all.

Warily I made my way backstage, feeling my way along, and crept into my dressing room and began to search for my suit. Even after the shattering experience at the gate, conflict was still raging between my common sense and my vanity—and vanity was winning out. But just as I began to get undressed Al burst into my room.

"She's coming!" he announced, waving something yellow in front of me. "Marie says she will come."

Marie was a girl who had tried riding for a short time in 1929 but had been persuaded to give up after a series of injuries culminating in a broken collarbone. She was a girl who had an amazing amount of courage but lacked real skill for riding diving horses. Although she was hardly an ideal substitute, Al (who had been having a rough time with me and my hardheaded insistence on riding when he felt I shouldn't) was relieved to get anyone at all. I didn't share his reaction. He had wired her without my knowledge, and the news of a substitute brought tears to my eyes. This blow to my pride was more severe than physical pain. In the eight years I had been riding I had never once needed a substitute, and with each season my pride in my stamina and ability had grown.

Al then told me that Mr. Endicott had heard of my trouble and had telephoned to say that the act could be canceled until Marie arrived. But I said I was going to ride anyway. It was Sunday and thousands of people swarmed on the pier. They expected to see a rider on the diving horse, and I was not going to disappoint them. A few more rides, I argued, couldn't make much difference. Al reluctantly agreed to let me ride. He left, saying, "All right, but this is the last day."

My only concession to my impaired vision was in the choice of a horse. Usually we worked the two horses alternately, but since I had discovered that dark objects showed up better in daylight and light ones better at night I asked that Klatawah be used during the day and Red Lips that night. There was some commotion among the water-sports gang when they heard I was going to continue riding until Marie could get there, because they thought Al was making me do it. That false notion was quashed quickly via Arnette. She delivered a message to them from me saying that I was riding at my own insistence, not Al's.

Later that afternoon at the top of the tower, as I waited for Klatawah's dark form to loom up in the vague grayness, my eyes filled with tears. The next time Klatawah made a dive I would not be riding him. I struggled sadly through the rest of the Sunday performances.

The following day brought Marie, and Al and I finally went to a doctor. He was considered to be one of the best eye specialists in that part of the country. After I had explained my accident and subsequent developments, he examined my eyes. He told me that the impact of the water had broken tiny blood vessels in my eyes and that the physical exertion of each ride thereafter had increased this internal hemorrhage to the point where more blood had accumulated than could be absorbed. The unabsorbed blood had clotted and began to detach my retinas.

The term "detached retina" meant nothing to me until he explained that the eye has three layers—the sclera, the choroid, and the retina—which lie one on top of the other, somewhat like the skin of an onion. The retina is the inner one and corresponds to the film in a camera. The blood clots had slipped between the choroid and retina and worked the retina loose, the way sand behind wallpaper will eventually work the wallpaper loose from the wall.

He pulled no punches in explaining how badly my eyes were injured, saying that he could not impress on me too strongly their serious condition. "I shall do everything within my power," he said, "to restore the sight in your right eye, but the state of your left eye seems utterly hopeless." He explained that apparently the retina of my left eye was completely smashed, but the retina of the right eye was still only partially detached. He warned me that hope for the right one was slight, however, because of limited medical knowledge in treating detached retinas.

The implication of blindness was horrifying. Indeed, the doctor's suggestion produced a sense of shock so profound that a part of my mind seemed to stop functioning, and the terrified thoughts that had scampered through my brain at the first realization of the possibility of my becoming permanently and totally blind were put away into some inner fastness and I refused to let them out.

"He's only trying to frighten me into being a docile patient," I told myself. "He doesn't really mean it." I clung to this rationalization as I followed a nurse down a corridor and into a room where she helped to undress me. So within a matter of hours I was snatched from a life filled with excitement and action to the monotony of a hospital bed.

Thirteen

The clinic was a small private hospital used solely for eye cases, for, as the doctor explained, "My patients are seldom ill and so they become restless when subjected to the strict routine of a general hospital. I find it much better to have them here where they may have company whenever they please."

His attitude was fortunate for me, since all the people I knew in Atlantic City were in show business and, owing to the schedule of their performances, would have found it difficult to come to see me during regular hospital visiting hours.

The room assigned to me was as austere as any ordinary hospital room. It had a bleak cleanliness which no amount of flowers or company ever completely abolished. I felt overwhelmed by its atmosphere as I slipped into bed. To Al, who appeared later with my things, I complained, "I never felt better in my life, and to be lying idle in bed seems the silliest thing in the world."

"You know what the doctor said," he replied.

"Yes, I know, and I'm going to try to co-operate, but I'll hate every minute of it, so please come whenever you can and tell everyone else to."

Al had no sooner left the room that day than I fell asleep. For the next three days I slept almost constantly, waking only for medical treatment, food, and visitors. I had not been aware of being either tired or sleepy before going to the hospital, and I think now that this overpowering urge to sleep was a psychological attempt on my part to escape the dismal picture the doctor had painted. Whatever its cause, after those three days I was surfeited and never again slept so solidly and continuously. Later I often prayed for the ability to sleep in order to pass away endless hours of monotony, but sleep would no longer come.

The worst part of those early days in the clinic was that I had to lie perfectly still. This was to allow the fluids and blood clots in my eyes to be absorbed so the doctor could better calculate the extent of the damage before attempting to operate. In the complete immobility of my body lay the only hope of saving my eyesight. I could move my arms up and down if I went about it very cautiously, but every other part of me had to remain like stone.

It is impossible to describe the agony of being absolutely still when you are perfectly well and accustomed to moving constantly. Muscles seem to shriek for movement, and nerves appear to be on top of the skin. There is no chance to relieve pressure on any part of the body, with the result that areas that press constantly on the mattress become desperately sore.

I was allowed no pillows; my head lay flat on the bed, and the back of it became so sore I could have cried. Having an unusually high curve in my back made my spine hurt even more than the rest of my body. They tried relieving the pressure there by means of a small air pillow shaped like a doughnut, but this was no cure. It merely lessened the ache.

I was not allowed to comb my hair or brush my teeth or get up to go to the bathroom. I hated all the restrictions, but the bedpan was the worst. Overwhelmed by the desire to get up and go to the bathroom by myself, I dreamed one night that I did but that I had no sooner got there than the doctor found me and gave me such a tongue-lashing that I flew back to bed.

It occurred to me that throwing a fit would be a relief from the tedium, but common sense prevented such an indulgence. I knew that throwing a fit would be for effect alone and that the effect would serve no purpose, so I told myself that I could hold on and would hold on in order to give myself every possible chance of regaining my sight.

The doctor checked my eyes every day and, on the fourth one, decided to operate. Before he left my room he explained the object of the operation and how it would be performed.

"It will not be painful," he went on. "I will put some drops in your eyes, and after a moment the surrounding tissue will begin to feel dead. Then I'll put an anesthetic into the lids with a needle, but you'll only feel a little pricking. This anesthetic will deaden not only the tissue around the eyeball but the eyeball itself. Once it has taken effect, you will feel nothing at all."

So far the doctor had never lied to me and I was confident I would feel no pain. I didn't, but even so the operation was a grueling business, and when it was over I was covered with sweat. My only sensory experience during the entire operation was the smell of burning flesh, which, as my nurse later explained, had occurred when the doctor cauterized the choroid.

First the doctor grasped the eyeball, she said, with a special instrument and twisted the eye around in the socket to expose the back of it. Then with a diathermy needle he pierced the eyeball to the depth of the retina.

When the needle reached a point precisely between the choroid and retina he cauterized a little spot, then another and another and another in a half-moon shape, so that when the cauterized places healed they would cause scar tissue to form and thus reattach the retina to the choroid. It was actually like gluing it back with scar tissue.

If the operation proved successful (as it did about fifty per cent of the time), some impairment of vision would result, but usually very little. My chances were less than fifty-fifty, however, because the retina was so badly damaged. Though no one had actually said so, I knew it would be a miracle if the operation was successful.

With the operation over, I had to lie still again, this time not for days but for three to four weeks, and the doctor warned me that immobility was even more important now than it had been before. If I couldn't manage it on my own, he said, he would put sandbags around me. I loathed the idea of being sandbagged and promised to keep very quiet.

Since I was not permitted to raise my head, the nurse, Mrs. Davis, fed me. From the beginning my greatest problem in connection with eating was timing. If I opened my mouth and the food wasn't immediately crammed in I began to feel the way a fish looks with its jaw agape. But if I hurriedly closed my mouth the nurse invariably said, "Open." No matter how hard I tried, we seemed to be continually working at cross purposes, and the results were often frustrating.

There was also a physical sensation connected with the act of chewing which bothered me considerably. All my Me I had chewed my food slowly and thoroughly, but now I began to wish I could swallow it whole. The act of chewing made the back of my head rub against the mattress, and this, in turn, made me conscious of the slow rhythmic motion of my jaw. Once my attention was riveted on it, it seemed as if my jaw began to grow, expanding in size with every successive chew until it was swollen alarmingly. Although I knew perfectly well this was not so, I could not help wondering if I looked as ridiculous as I felt.

I was allowed no salt on my food and was given very little liquid—one cup of coffee, one glass of iced tea, and about half a glass of water each day. It was a grim menu, and only once did something happen to brighten my mealtime.

That day the nurse from next door, who was going off duty, came by to visit Mrs. Davis, who had just finished feeding me my lunch. The lunch tray—containing the remains of an assortment of vegetables, watery potatoes, and some unidentified ground meat—was still on the table.

"Why didn't you give her the green pepper the meat was stuffed in?" the other nurse wanted to know.

"Because," said Mrs. Davis, "I don't like it"

For hours and hours, lacking all company but my own and occasionally the nurse's, I often retreated into my thoughts to escape present reality, taking shelter in some memory. Sometimes scenes passed in review before me like floats in a parade and I would lie there watching them as if from a special balcony. Most were transitory and fragmentary, but a few that were strong and clear came back not once but several times to reimpress themselves. The memory that kept returning with the greatest persistence was something that happened when I was fourteen years old.

In my mind's eye I saw a group of children lounging languidly on the end of a small pier extending out into the liquid amber of St. Johns River. A few huge white clouds drifted overhead like lazy vagabonds, and at the shoreline great masses of lavender water hyacinths floated on the undulating surface of the water. A blazing August sun descended toward the west. The children lingered because it was pleasant with the water lapping softly against the pilings and they were enjoying one another's company. Idly chatting of this and that, they somehow stumbled on the subject of death. As the discussion developed, a question was posed: since everybody had to die eventually, what age would be best?

Someone said she didn't want to die until she was ninety; someone else said fifty. There were various other choices offered simultaneously, but one voice rose above the rest. "I want to die when I'm twenty-seven," it said—and I recognized the voice as mine.

This recurring memory continued to frighten me, for I had just turned twenty-seven and, whatever I had said in the past, I did not wish to die. Strange that I had chosen that age, wasn't it, or that I remembered it now? Was the remembering significant? Had I made an irrevocable choice?

I would no sooner ask these questions than I'd assure myself they were nonsense and that I was being foolish. Then my healthy supply of common sense would return to back me up—until the next time that compelling scene forced its way into my consciousness.

Another scene was almost as vivid. In this one a woman was sitting in a chair, wearing a selfish, petulant expression. A family group moved around her, and whenever one of them got in her shadow they seemed to shrink.

This woman was a friend of my mother's and a rampant hypochondriac. She made her whole family unhappy with her ceaseless complaints; she claimed to suffer from a little of everything. She never lifted a hand to help with the housework, not even such chores as mending, using the excuse of her "illness."

I made a resolution then which I had never forgotten: no matter what happened to me, I would never blight the lives of those around me by constant complaining. Now I could only hope that should circumstance change my life and force me, even though authentically, into a situation similar to hers I would have the courage to stick by my pledge.

Company helped to distract me from introspection, but unfortunately I didn't have it often. All our friends at the pier were then doing as many as five performances a day, for I went to the hospital at the height of the season. Almost the only regular visitors I had were Arnette and Al, who somehow managed to turn up between their appearances. They could never stay long. For the short time they were there I eagerly fired questions at them. Afterward I clung to every little detail of what was going on at the pier in order to have something aside from myself to think about.

They both reported that all was not well. Marie's comeback was not proving a success, and Al didn't know how much longer she would continue to ride. She had begun on Monday and by Friday had thrown in the sponge as far as riding Red Lips was concerned. "Not that I blame her," Al said, "because Red is tough to ride and she just hasn't got what it takes. I'm not trying to be funny when I say she's a walking, talking bruise. She's black and blue from head to toe, and many of the bruises have swelled, making her look knobby and out of shape."

"How does she get along with Klatawah?"

"Oh, she says shell ride him if I want her to, but I think she wishes she didn't have to ride any horse again as long as she lives."

"What are you going to do about a rider for Red?"

"I've been thinking about Marty. You know he's often said he'd like to ride, so tonight when Marie announced she had had enough of Red I asked him if he would be willing to try and he agreed. We're going out early in the morning to give him a couple of trial rides from the low tower. I think he'll get along all right because his strength will go a long way toward making up for his lack of experience."

Marty sounded like a good idea to me. He was small but extremely husky and a trained athlete. During the winter he worked as a physical education instructor in one of the New York high schools; in the summer he became one of the water-sports gang, riding aquaplanes and driving motor-boats.

He began practice the next day, but a week passed before he was able to ride Red out of the tank. "I don't know what I'm going to do about Red," Al said. "He dives as if he were dumping these new riders on purpose. Which may be the key to the problem. After all, you've been his only rider up until now."

Of course the idea that Red Lips preferred me to anyone else pleased me immensely. Nevertheless, if he was deliberately trying to knock the riders off he had to be stopped.

"Maybe if you'd have Marty pal up to him it would help. You know how Red loves attention. Suggest that Marty go around to his stall between performances and talk to him and take him a carrot or an apple. And tell Marty to come and see me when he gets a chance. I think I can come up with some advice that may help him."

Marty didn't waste any time getting himself over to the hospital. He was there the next morning.

"I hear you've been having some trouble," I said.

"Boy, I'll say I have! I don't do anything with that animal." And then he proceeded to tell me in great and vivid detail what had been happening. By the time he finished I had figured out part of his trouble.

"You're not holding your weight back," I said. "On a horse that makes a plunge dive your position is less important, but on Red you must be properly balanced. Don't duck until you're ready to hit the water. That's important too. I think if you'll try just those two things you'll find you can handle him. You may even find it's fun."

"Lady," Marty said dryly, "I used to think it would be fun when I watched you doing it, but now I'm telling you that all I'm doing it for is the dough." Marty's motives might have been mercenary, but they didn't interfere with his learning, for Al reported a few days later that Red Lips was slowly yielding to Marty's overtures of friendship and that in the meantime Marty was getting enough experience on him at least to get by.

Al had scarcely straightened out the crisis over Red when another problem arose. Early one afternoon Arnette rushed into my room so out of breath from running she could hardly talk.

"Marie is gone!" she gasped. "When we got to the pier today Al had a note from her. It said that she had either flu or pneumonia and was going home!"

"Pneumonia?" I said. "But she rode last night, didn't she?"

"Yes," Arnette replied, "but she's had a cold for two or three days and she's pretty banged up, so I guess she just decided she didn't want to take it any longer. Anyway, she's gone." She paused for a minute, still panting. "Al's going to need another rider," she said. "How about me?"

According to Al, Arnette had been badgering him ever since I had had to quit but, aware of my feelings, he had refused to listen.

"That's why I'm here," she went on. "I've just finished my first show and have to run right back, but I wanted to get over here ahead of Al so that I could ask you to ask him to let me ride. I think he'd do it for you."

In the moment after she stopped speaking every bad ride she had ever made flashed across my mind: the sideways take-offs, the near somersaults, the almost-too-late duck of the head. I recalled the succession of charley horses she had had up the inside of both thighs because she had never learned to take advantage of the "shock-absorber" inner tube behind a horse's forequarters, which gives a rider something to brace her knees against just before bitting the water.

"Why do you want to dive?" I asked. "I've seen you so crippled you could hardly walk."

"Because I love it," she said, "just the way you do. I love the horses and the excitement and people making a fuss over me. I just love it, that's all."

How could I argue? That night when Al came I consulted with him about letting Arnette ride. "I've been going over her performances in my mind," I said, "trying to figure out what's wrong, and I think maybe I've got it. Arnette is ambidextrous but favors her left hand. When I taught her to ride I taught her from the standpoint of a right-handed person and told her to always duck to the right. Maybe if she tried ducking to the left she'd find it more natural and she could ride much better. Why don't you start her again with a couple of rides from the low tower to see how it goes and, if she does all right, have her try a dive from the high tower?"

The next night when both of them came to see me after the last performance they were in high spirits. Al said, "I think you've found the secret. Her rides were perfect!"

"It was the first time I've ever felt completely right and comfortable," Arnette said. "Why didn't you think of it before?"

Fourteen

For three weeks after my operation the doctor checked my eyes every day. During the examination he never said anything to me. Each time he finished with the words, "That's fine," and directed the nurse to put the bandages back on. But I suspected that things weren't fine. Actually it seemed to me that the little sight I had had when I came to the hospital had. grown steadily dimmer and was now threatening to disappear entirely.

Finally the doctor admitted that my sight was ebbing away. At this crucial and critical point (for time was running out) he explained that he was going to attempt a last desperation measure. The treatment involved injecting a needle into the eye and pumping air through it into the cavity in front of the retina. The theory was that if enough pressure could be exerted it might press the retina back against the choroid and help to reattach it.

With this operation, the doctor warned me, I would have some pain, but he could not possibly have made me understand how painful it would be. Immediately after the injection I felt nothing, but in a minute the pain built up until it seemed to fill the whole side of my head. I had never known anything so intense in my life. It taught me the real meaning of "excruciating." Still, when the treatment didn't work the first time, I was willing to have him try it again because I realized this was my last chance. I went through the same process. It proved unsuccessful. I knew I must face the truth.

Until now I had forced all my frightened thoughts into the recesses of my brain. Only by hiding them had I been able to eat, sleep occasionally, and talk to those around me with some semblance of a normal manner, but I was never completely free of those lurking thoughts. Among them was something I refused to name.

All along, the smoky grayness that had obscured my vision when I entered the hospital had been darkening, and now I found myself enveloped in folds of soft black velvet. As complete as the darkness was, I still managed to ignore the nameless terror. I told myself that the doctor hadn't said my sight was gone, so perhaps I was mistaken; but one morning, as I lay looking into infinite blackness, a spot of light no larger than a pearl suddenly appeared. It possessed a radiant phosphorescent glow, and I stared at it in surprise. I had had no sensation of light for so long. What did it mean?

As I stared it seemed to advance and expand and grow larger and assume the form of a word, but I had no sooner realized it was a word than a dread took possession of me, warning me not to read it.

Of course this spot of light with the word it formed was a phenomenon of the mind, but it seemed so real that I actually closed my eyes both physically and mentally against it. I could not continue to disregard it, however, for as soon as I opened my eyes the spot would appear again, grow larger, and advance. This happened several times, until I was finally compelled to read it. I realized it would not go away. As the spot appeared, small and glowing against the darkness, I watched breathlessly. Steadily it advanced and expanded until the letters were enormous and seemed to be rushing at me with great speed. Then it was upon me and I read the word blind.

I was so dazzled by the radiance and the overwhelming size of the letters that stood before me, burning and blazing like fire, that I closed my eyes for a moment and released a deep sigh. For a moment I lay there feeling nothing, knowing only that I had faced the thing I had been trying so desperately to escape. The something I had wanted so desperately to remain nameless had been given a name.

After that my first reaction was a sense of relief. It was no longer necessary to run. In place of running I could begin to think, but thinking released the cowardly thoughts I had kept hidden. Like insects trapped in a room, they flew around my brain, beating their wings in a vain attempt to escape. They became more and more panic-stricken and, to a monotonous refrain of "I don't believe it! It isn't true!" finally exhausted themselves.

After I rested a bit, logic began to restore order out of chaos, and a small voice heretofore unheard in the uproar said, "You know you'll never see again. Will you let it ruin your life?"

Until then life had not been exactly easy, but I had hurdled one problem after another without breaking my stride. Now, with the impact of a person running in the dark, I had crashed into a wall. The violence had thrown me back and left me stunned and helpless. As I slowly recovered from the shock I began to realize this wall (intangible though it was, utterly lacking in material substance) as possessing the quality of granite. Indeed my imaginary wall presented a barrier much more formidable than a real one, because a real one could be torn down. My wall seemed indestructible.

This was a dark time for me, the darkest I was to know, for I had to face the knowledge of my blindness alone. Al and Arnette had been duly warned, but they did not yet realize that now all hope was gone. When I was struck by what blindness meant, with all its implications, I could not avoid being overwhelmed at a prospect of empty, fruitless years awaiting me. How could I face them? What would I do?

Then one day as I struggled with my thoughts of a future that must be faced in darkness a strange thing happened. As I lay there in the hospital, the silence around me seemed to deepen and become amplified. In the heart of this silence, seemingly at its very core, there was a feeling of presence. How else shall I describe it? There are no words. I can only say that I knew as emphatically as we know very few things in life that I was in the presence of God.

The knowledge wasn't frightening. On the contrary, it was deeply reassuring. It contained peace and majesty and an infinity of comfort.

Lost for a moment in its vastness, I thought and heard nothing. Then the quiet ebbed away as unobtrusively as it had come and I discovered that in some totally inexplicable manner I had received a blessing. It was as if God had laid His hand on my shoulder and said, "Don't be afraid. You will see."

It took a while for me to absorb this experience, since it struck at the very bedrock of my existence, but when I attempted an interpretation I concluded that the promise had not meant the restoration of my physical sight. What God was promising was greater mental vision to compensate for the loss of eyesight. If I could believe this, then I was well content. I told myself I would rather have an intelligent brain, capable of greater mental vision behind eyes that were sightless, than a stupid brain behind eyes that could see.

With this understanding of God's promise to strengthen me I prayed for the courage to hold firmly to my resolution, made so long ago, never to become a burden to those around me. Next I began to catalogue my personal assets; if I were to succeed in climbing the wall that stood before me I would need every asset I could muster.

Fifteen

I began to give my attention to what was going on around me, trying to interpret the information which my other senses were pouring into my mind in an unabating stream. Sounds, odors, tastes, forms, and textures were uniting, it seemed, in an effort to present the world around me as it had always been.

I was delighted to find that nothing had changed. Food still tasted the same; things smelled as good or as bad; form and texture were wonderfully reassuring when I ran my hands over objects on the table beside my bed. And sounds? I was startled to find that many sounds were already as familiar to my ears as the actions that produced them had been familiar to my eyes; I had just never been consciously aware of these sounds.

Further observation taught me that nearly all activity within the hospital tended to produce definite sound patterns. In the beginning, collecting different sounds and then transforming them into a mental picture was laborious, but my mind gained speed with practice and the process became automatic. The realization of what all my other senses could do to help me was wonderful. It gave me confidence in my own resource and enabled me to make an important decision before I left the hospital.

After considering the matter from every angle I decided that the best strategy I could adopt would be to treat my blindness as if it were a minor detail rather than a major catastrophe. I would thus be turning the tables on my handicap; in fact, striking at its very potency. I was careful, however, not to delude myself; the way would not be easy. Although I was over the wall, there was a wilderness beyond it, one totally unknown to me, and I would have to remind myself constantly that the manner in which I traveled through this wilderness depended a great deal on my attitude.

Once I was home, I insisted with a fervor so intense as to verge on passion, that I be allowed to do as many things for myself as possible. My loss of sight had aroused the sympathy of everyone close to me, and their natural reaction was to wait on me hand and foot. Gently but firmly I refused to accept most of their services, for I realized the importance of building a firm foundation of self-reliance right from the start. The habit of being waited on could grow into a dangerous one, possibly weakening and eventually conquering my determination to do it alone.

My first victory in this direction had to do with bathing. For some reason (perhaps he feared an accident), the doctor had suggested that I have someone bathe me, so Arnette appointed herself to perform this operation. I stood it for a couple of days and then had had enough. "What in the world is to keep me from rubbing a washcloth over my own face and back?" I said. "This babying is nonsense. I'm not crippled."

The next night, before going to bed, I got my towel and washcloth and the soap and placed them within reach of the tub. Then I laid out my night clothes and proceeded to fill the tub with water. After that I got in and bathed and that's all there was to it. This taught me a lesson I was to keep on learning over and over again—if you don't know whether you can do it or not, try it and see.

After my siege in the hospital I was sick to death of having someone feed me and, from the moment I returned home, would allow no more of that. I let Al cut up my meat because he said it made him nervous to watch my efforts with a knife. Beyond that, all he did was place the vegetables on my plate and tell me where they were. The rest was up to me.

Some meals were not easy. One of the first dinners after I returned from the hospital included a bowl of soup. I had thought in advance that nothing could be simpler than soup. There was nothing to cut, untangle, or skewer; just the soup, the spoon, and my mouth. But, without fail, somewhere en route to my mouth from the bowl the liquid spilled out of the spoon and back into the bowl. The difficulty, I discovered, was that I hadn't the slightest notion of how to keep the spoon on a level. Any way I tried to tip it to bring it to an even keel proved wrong. For a long time thereafter the spoon remained empty better than half the time. I would have surely starved to death if I had had to live on soup.

There were also canned peaches. The blind person doesn't need a spoon; he needs a trap. One night I kept trying to get them into the spoon as they slipped and flipped and flopped like a bunch of live goldfish, and suddenly I heard Al say, "It isn't as easy as you thought, is it?"

Thinking he was referring to my awkwardness, I looked up and started to answer, but before I could speak Arnette said, "No, it certainly isn't." Then she explained to me, "I watched you struggling with those peaches and wondered why you were having such a time. I closed my eyes and now I know."

If I had been willing to dispense with good table manners, feeding myself would have been much easier, but I had set a fairly high standard for myself, which added to my difficulties. I had resolved to eat as properly as I had done when I could see, or possibly even a bit more properly. Above all, I would not allow myself to eat with my hands. Once or twice I yielded to the temptation to pick up a piece of pie or cake instead of eating it with a fork but found I didn't enjoy it. I had to use the tip of a left finger to guide things onto my fork or the tip of a right finger to judge the depth or heat of Liquid in a glass or cup, but I made certain these motions were brief and unobtrusive, for I would sooner have died than appear boorish.

Occasionally Al sneaked in some help without my knowledge, but whenever I caught him I displayed so much anger that he didn't try again— at least for a while. I realized he was helping me one day when my fork banged down on his. He had been scraping food together on my plate to make it easier for me to find the pieces, but I told him I'd rather find them myself than have him piling up my food. It made me feel like a four-year-old and I didn't like it.

I was equally stubborn about moving around the house without the use of a stick. In the beginning this insistence achieved painful results, for my judgment of direction and distance was very poor and I constantly banged and bumped into all sorts of sharp-edged obstacles—open doors and doorframes and pieces of furniture—and usually hit them hard, because I had vowed to blunder into things rather than creep about as if I were afraid. Although I had never paid much attention to blind people, my one deep impression of them was the uncertain way they moved, and I wanted to avoid developing that characteristic. The more confidently I moved and the more I managed for myself, the less attention I would attract to my blindness. I hated the idea of using it to win special compensations.

My intimate associates readily grasped the idea of my wish for independence and co-operated, but I had scarcely launched myself on this program when I discovered a lack of understanding on the part of casual acquaintances. This was particularly true of those who let sentiment rule reason. To refuse the services of such overly solicitous friends required a great deal of tact and patience, for some of them were extremely persistent. As a matter of fact, as my ability to do things myself increased they actually seemed to resent it. After a while I gave in and let them perform small services which I could perfectly well have done for myself, for it made them happier or at least seemed to confirm their impressions of what a blind person should be.

This attitude of overprotection toward the blind, not infrequent among the sighted, often can be more of a handicap than blindness itself, and one of its most damaging aspects is the continual effort to help the blind person physically at the expense of the blind person's feelings.

This was amply illustrated by an occurrence one day shortly after I came home. A friend who lived next door dropped in one morning to say hello and found me busily engaged in making my bed for the first time. I refused the help offered, telling her I wanted to learn to do it myself, and we chatted while I finished. I asked her how it looked and she claimed it looked fine. After she left, Arnette came in and said, "You've got the bedspread on upside down."

"Why didn't she tell me?" I said furiously.

"She said she didn't want to hurt your feelings."

"But that's not helping me!" I retorted. "If somebody tells me something looks fine when it's a mess, how am I going to learn?"

Learning to do things was indeed difficult but not nearly so difficult as learning the patience it took to do them. Performing domestic tasks in the dark produces constant and infuriating frustrations. This reaction can be understandable to the sighted if they recall nights when they have gotten up in the dark and tried to accomplish some objective without turning on the light.

If it's merely finding the route to the bathroom, one may do very well, but if it's nose drops in a cabinet or a blanket on a closet shelf, the search becomes complicated. Even if one is absolutely certain of the location, there is still the unforeseen. Reaching for the nose drops turns over a box of boric acid; pulling down the blanket releases a cascade of boxes.

It is these constant incalculables that make the world of the blind so hazardous—these plus the fact that it takes two or three times longer to dress, for example, than it once did. Several personal factors entered into my case, however, so perhaps my difficulties in getting dressed were only enhanced by my blindness.

First of all, I am meticulous about my appearance. I have never been able to abide messy hair or a crooked stocking seam or a slip that showed. When I became blind, this feeling was intensified and, being uncertain of exactly how I looked, I took special pains. I loathed the thought of having some woman say to herself, "Poor thing. Her sweater is buttoned up crooked, but she can't help it. She can't see."

In contrast to my meticulous attitude on the subject of clothes was my hitherto scatterbrained nature. I had always found it difficult to keep my mind on the task at hand, preferring to let it amble off onto such matters as gravity or Rudolph Valentino. I often mislaid things or even forgot what I was doing. As a result, almost everything took me longer to do than it took anyone else, but now I had to get rid of this habit In fact, I had to fight it by making a special effort to concentrate on what I was doing, for if I did not I was hopelessly lost Should I let my mind wander for a second while putting on my powder, I was just as likely as not to set the box down someplace and then immediately turn it over, which of course meant more time spent cleaning it up. Fortunately I had a good memory, and as time went on I became more and more adept at putting it to work.

127

(Al always says that he marvels not so much that I finally made a satisfactory adjustment to blindness as that I have managed to live long enough to adjust to anything. In this there is some truth, but there is more truth in the maxim which I devised personally: "Blindness is not so much a tragedy as it is a damn nuisance.")

Another factor having to do with appearance which concerned me greatly was the desire to avoid falling into the habit of letting my face assume, by gradual stages, the appearance of a death mask. I wanted my face to be warm and alive, a part of the living world around me. I had not lost control of my eye muscles; the eyes themselves were still clear and of normal shape, and I could move them in any direction I choose. Outwardly they did not in any way evidence the fact of their blindness, so I knew that if I concentrated on keeping my expression lively there was no reason that it should ever become wooden.

I encountered one difficulty, however. I was told that for some inexplicable reason I had a tendency to focus upward when I looked at someone, and yet when I focused my eyes lower I felt as if I were looking at the ground. This made me uncomfortable, since I was afraid unsuspecting people might think I was trying to avoid their eyes. I had always made a point to look directly at people when talking to them and wanted to continue to do so. Consciously remembering to keep my eyes properly focused while trying to concentrate on the conversation was at first extremely tricky. When I bent my mind to focusing, I lost track of what was being said, and if I became too engrossed in words I forgot to shift my eyes. It was a difficult situation which I never resolved to my own satisfaction, but I have gradually become more adept.

Sometimes, of course, I was lonely. I had occasional visitors, but Al and Arnette were home only at night after the last performance, aside from hurried meals. My one steady companion was our cook, Mrs. Van Myers.

Al had hired Mrs. Van Myers as soon as he knew I was coming out of the hospital. While I was gone from the apartment he and Arnette had eaten in restaurants, but they both agreed that it would be simpler for me and for all of us to have our meals at home once I was back. He got in touch with an employment agency, and the result was Van Myers.

She was a mountain of a woman, weighing, she admitted, 250 pounds. She had the tread of a mastodon, a deep and hearty laugh, and a wheezing breath which seemed to be drawn through a straw from somewhere down near the feet. Her principal hobby was beating the drum and singing with the Salvation Army. Actually she was a blessing. Not only was she a good cook, but she loved to talk and often kept me entertained for hours with stories about her relatives. From time to time even she would lapse into silence during the day, and it was always ominously quiet after she left in the evening.

When alone, I fell into the habit of reciting poetry or singing aloud to myself. I don't have much of a voice, and I remembered only a little poetry, so these concerts were usually short-lived. Why we didn't get a radio, I don't know. We had had one in California but sold it when we left, for in those days radios were formidable-sized objects and difficult to move. Perhaps this was why it didn't occur to any of us to get another one. We would be leaving Atlantic City as soon as the season was over and subconsciously must have concluded we would have had to sell a radio within a few weeks of the purchase.

One break in the monotony of my apartment-bound life was provided by friends who now and then came by to visit or take me out for a walk. Usually they were inexperienced in guiding a blind person, their judgment of space or timing being no better than mine, with results that were sometimes near disastrous. Quite unintentionally they would often carefully lead me into holes in the sidewalk, and one day a well-meaning friend guided me right up to an open casement window, the point of which struck me in the eye. It hurt so badly I fainted, but when I came to I was able to tell her that, at least temporarily, she had made me see. All kinds of colored pinwheels and skyrockets zoomed around for a minute.

The difficulty was compounded by my method of navigation; I had a tendency to sway away from whoever was accompanying me. Al, in particular, found this annoying. We would be walking straight ahead, Al holding onto the upper part of my arm, propelling me forward (which, though we hadn't been told then, was the exact opposite of the manner in which a blind person should be steered; I should have taken his arm and let him lead, not jockey me), when I would suddenly pull away from him and list to one side.

"Why do you do that?" he would ask, as if I had done it on purpose.

"I don't know," I would reply. And for a long time I didn't. Later I realized it was because I had no horizon to keep me on an even keel. What I was experiencing was a slight case of vertigo, that inner-ear confusion familiar to pilots when flying in a fog. At such times one's sense of what is up and what is down is completely confused because he has no line in front of him to serve as a level.

But among the odds and the ends of living which put new strains and restrictions on me, the worst was not being able to read. I had always been a bookworm and was wild to learn Braille, but there was no school for the blind in Atlantic City. I would have to wait until the season was over and go to the one in Philadelphia. Al would have time then to take me back and forth from Lorena's farm in Quakertown, where we planned to winter. In the meantime friends tried to fill the gap by reading aloud to me, but their enthusiasm for the project speedily waned. Not that I blamed them. Never having enjoyed reading aloud to anyone, I did not wonder that they didn't enjoy reading aloud to me.

One day, weary of Mrs. Van Myers' constant rumble (by then I had heard all the tales of her relatives) and desperate for something to do, I decided to iron. I had been completely dependent on someone else for this job. It fell to Arnette, who was so busy at the pier that I disliked her having to iron my clothes in addition to her own. I had been afraid to try my luck for fear that I might burn myself. Not only that, I doubted my ability to do it without ironing wrinkles into everything.

To my complete surprise, I found it quite easy. My fingers relayed almost all the information that previously had been provided by my eyes, and I managed ruffles and tucks as if I had been using the touch system for years.

Surely the value of the sense of touch can hardly be overestimated. I have often wondered what Helen Keller would have done if that, too, had been denied her. The fingers are, after all, extensions of the eyes and describe to the blind what they can neither see nor hear. Texture, temperature, solidity. How else would a blind person tell? I found out how important it was one day when I put on rubber gloves to do some washing. Immediately I felt as if I had lost my sight all over again and quickly I took them off. The effect was almost frightening.

Naturally this sense was most important when I was in strange surroundings. When we went visiting in a house I had never entered while I was sighted, I could never relax and join in the conversation until I had achieved some measure of orientation. In a new place I had an unnerving feeling that I was looking at the wrong things and would find myself growing uneasy and would have an overwhelming urge to leave. To overcome this feeling I began to ask questions. If my hosts were casual acquaintances I simply requested a description of the room, including the placement of most of its contents, but if I knew them well and anticipated future visits in their home I would ask them to show me around the room and let me familiarize myself with it by touching shelves and tables and doors. When I had done so I could settle down to enjoy their company.

The only time I resisted the use of touch was when it came to identifying people. I could not bring myself to examine their faces with my fingers, no matter how much I wished to know what they looked like. That would have been far too personal, an invasion of their privacy, so I depended on others for facial descriptions, although the descriptions usually were disappointingly inadequate.

I was amazed to find how generally inadequate most people's powers of observation were. Either that or they did not know how to describe what they saw. I would ask, "What does Carol look like?" and someone would answer, "She's tall."

"What else?" I would say eagerly.

"She has brown eyes and dark hair."

Unless I persisted, little more would be forthcoming. Only later, through some circumstance or other, would I learn that Carol had a widow's peak, that her eyes were lively, that she stood head-high to Red Lips, and that she had a scar on her chin. Any one of these things would have helped to give me a definite idea of what Carol looked like, but none of this information came from direct questioning.

Many people cling to the belief that the loss of sight stimulates the other senses, particularly the sense of hearing, but I did not find this to be true. A blind person learns to listen closely. Without the loss of sight, hearing is secondary and merely adds another dimension, but when the sight goes the sense of hearing really comes into its own and translates admirably. I have said that while I was still in the hospital it was a great source of encouragement and comfort to me to find that my other senses were taking over. I noticed this with regard to my hearing in the very beginning and often demonstrated it unconsciously.

One day Arnette brought some mending to do while she visited me. After a while I asked her what she was sewing.

"How did you know I was sewing?" she countered, amazement apparent in her voice.

"Because I heard the sound of the thread being pulled through the cloth," I replied, "and the snip of the scissors."

If I had been able to see I would hardly have been conscious of these sounds, but, as it was, they were unmistakable. Another time Al raced into the room in a rush between performances. He had been there only a few minutes when he looked at his watch.

"What time is it?" I asked.

"How did you know I looked at my watch?" he said, the same tone of astonishment in his voice as had been in Arnette's. "I didn't make a sound!"

"That's what you think. I heard the rustle of the material when you put your hand in your pocket. I heard the faint ticking when you took it out. It got louder as you held it up to look at it and got fainter when you put it away."

The action of a woman digging in her purse to find a lipstick, of someone pulling out a pack of cigarettes and extracting one, of uncapping or screwing on the top of a fountain pen—all these actions had and have certain individual sounds, many of them forming definite patterns. I demonstrated the business of pattern to Al by describing to him what we were going to have for dinner. (This after Mrs. Van Myers left and he was doing the cooking.) I nearly floored him when I diagnosed mashed potatoes.

"But how in the world could you know that?" he asked. "You certainly couldn't smell them. You were halfway across the room."

"I heard the sack rustle," I said, "when you got them out. I heard the sound of the big pan when you set it down on the drainboard. You always use the big pan when you boil potatoes, and it has a deeper voice than the others. Later I heard you open the drawer and get something out. When you put it down it had a dull metallic sound, and I knew it was the masher."

Most cherished of all my faculties however—over sound, over touch, over smell—was memory. During the first months of my blindness people used to ask, "How do you feel about losing your sight? Don't you miss it more than you would have if you hadn't been blind all your life?"

The answer to that one has always been, "You can't miss what you never had," but I couldn't use this answer because it seemed to me to have a built-in weakness. Perhaps you can't truly miss what you have never had; given imagination, however, you can be filled with a yearning to possess what you have never possessed. I found my reply to their question after comparing people who were born blind and those who were blinded later. The answer was, "I wouldn't take all the money in the world for once having been able to see."

How can it ever be possible to describe to a person blind from birth the color red? No matter what you say or do, you cannot convey it. Yet in my case, all a person had to say was "red" and immediately the color flashed across my mind; like Mother's cannas along the back-yard fence; red like the ribbons we tied on Christmas packages; red like the dress I bought when I was sixteen which was supposed to make me wicked. All description is based on comparisons, and I had the basis for comparisons. Nothing could ever take it from me, and it is my most precious legacy.

I am rich in memory, and as long as I have it to rehearse and define I am not really blind.

Sixteen

Two weeks before we were due to leave Atlantic City a friend of mine who knew how I longed to learn Braille called to say that on a shopping trip to Philadelphia she had telephoned the School for the Blind and asked if they knew anyone in Atlantic City qualified to teach Braille. She had been given the name of a Miss Sadie Cohen.

I can never be grateful enough to my friend for having put me in touch with Miss Cohen, who proved to be a really remarkable teacher. She taught me the most advanced form of Braille in just twelve lessons. Many people who have been blind for years never learn to read any but the simplest form. This does not mean that I actually learned to read that quickly; it means that she showed me how the system worked so that I was able to practice it until I became facile at both reading and writing. Over all, this took several months.

Braille is a kind of shorthand that does not use actual letters but a series of dots to represent letters or particular words. The dots are made by means of a stylus, a thin, short piece of metal set into a knob which fits into the palm of the hand and very much resembles a sawed-off ice pick.

Miss Cohen began by explaining the principle of Braille and then, with her slate and stylus, punched out the twenty-six letters of the alphabet on the heavy cardboard of an egg carton, "Because," she explained, "it is easier in the beginning for the fingers to distinguish the dots or bumps on something heavier than Braille paper."

In addition to this cardboard she gave me a tiny square of wood containing two parallel lines of three holes each, with pegs to fit into them. The first row of holes was numbered one, three, and five, and the second row two, four, and six. This little block represented one cell on a Braille slate and was ideal to learn on, since it magnified many times the real cell on a slate.

I took the slate and the egg carton home with me and, by pushing the pegs into the holes of the block in all the various positions, soon learned the alphabet. That is to say, my brain did. My fingers learned much more slowly. I went over and over the letters time after time, trying to make them interpret to an impatiently waiting brain the word or letter the dots indicated.

Finally I thought I had mastered the alphabet sufficiently to try reading a book, so after we moved to Quakertown that winter I wrote the distribution center which furnished blind people in that area with Braille books and asked for a copy of *The Count of Monte Cristo*. They informed me that they were sending along the first volume of this story; there were fifteen others! Braille printing takes up a great deal of room, and only a small amount of copy can be put on a page, even though the pages are quite large. When a Braille book is spread out on a table it it is almost the size of a newspaper. The books are not heavy, however, since their paper is of a pulpy texture.

I began my reading eagerly, with my mind clear and willing to understand whatever the finger conveyed to it, but the finger was stupid and faltered time and again. Finally, in a completely instinctive gesture, I laid my forehead on the page and almost immediately seemed to be able to understand what the word or letter was. For a long time thereafter I continued to read in this fashion, until I was finally able to read as well sitting erect as I had with my brain to the page.

Being able to read helped pass the winter for me, as did a visit from Mother.

I had forbidden anyone to tell her about my being in the hospital until we were certain of the outcome, but only when I knew there was no hope had I permitted Arnette to write her. Even then I emphasized the fact that she was not to come yet; I wanted to get accustomed to doing things for myself before she saw me. I knew it was going to distress her, and I wanted to be as agile as I could in as many things as I could in order to relieve at least part of her concern. When I felt that I could do enough for myself to relieve her mind on this score I had Arnette invite her to come and stay with us at Lorena's.

Al went to meet Mother at the station the day she arrived and drove her to the farm. She came directly to where I was sitting in the living room, and when she kissed me I felt tears on her cheeks. During the next few minutes she hovered over me in a nervous, fluttery fashion, her maternal instinct obviously bent on helping and protecting her offspring; but, being balked by a condition which even her love could not change, she could do little but fuss over me. She seemed afraid that mention of my lost eyesight would make me unhappy, so she carefully avoided it, until finally, to ease the strain, I began to talk about it myself, telling her how it happened and how I felt about it.

After a bit she asked somewhat hesitantly, "Who dresses you, dear?"

That was old hat for me by this time. I laughed. "Why, I do it myself, Mother, and I have from the first. Come on and I'll show you." I led her upstairs to my room. "See," I said as I opened the drawers of my dressing table and chest, "I have fixed places for different articles. It's just a matter of remembering where each thing is stored."

Then I took her to the closet and explained how I recognized different dresses. "It's easy," I told her, lifting the sleeve of a dress. "This is my blue crepe, and I recognize it by the feel of the material, also because it has a boat-shaped neckline and is ornamented with French knots. It's the same with each one; my fingers identify them.

"I even put on my own make-up," I went on. "But when I've finished I usually ask someone how I look. No smears, smudges, or what not. As a matter of fact, dressing myself and caring for my clothes has become one of my easiest tasks."

By the time Mother left a week later I think she was convinced that, bad as it was for a twenty-seven-year-old girl to be blind for life, it might have been much worse.

If I persuaded her to this point of view, I did so without faking. And I sincerely agreed: my situation might have been much worse. It seems to me that everyone has to make adjustments to life, that we all have our limitations, but that if we are wise we do not make other people miserable by concentrating on these limitations. One of the fundamental responsibilities of every human being in his relationship with others is to create happiness, not destroy it. We also have responsibilities toward ourselves. The prime one is not to make ourselves miserable by dwelling on something we can do nothing about.

The full flower of this philosophy was not mine at the time, but the roots of it were there, and day by day I made myself act as I wished to believe. I never allowed myself the luxury of mourning over the loss of my sight, nor, indeed, had I any inclination to. I was too busy learning to live in a world entirely new to me and usually managed to think of it as a kind of adventure. Only one time in all the days and weeks and months after I lost my sight did I cry over this loss, and that was not because I was grieving but because I was frustrated.

One evening Lorena had some people over to play cards. I sat in the living room where they were, listening to the radio. As the evening wore on, the crowd grew noisier and I could not hear over their voices, so I turned the radio up. So high, apparently, that it annoyed Lorena. The outcome was a quarrel between us that was both deep and biting and in which both of us said things we shouldn't have.

As I ran out of the living room and up to my bedroom I began to cry. More than anything in the world I would have liked to be able to walk out of her house and never come back, but I couldn't because of my blindness. In this case it was my incapacity to behave as a normal person that caused my tears rather than any mourning over the loss of my sight.

Spring came finally, and when it did Al began to get ready for the new season. As he made the usual preparations I found myself growing more restless than I had been at any time since losing my sight. Thus far I had managed to fill my time with learning the basic essentials of living in a new world, but now I had mastered these essentials and was ready to move ahead. I needed something definite to occupy my mind and time; in fact, to justify my very existence. The mechanics of existence were no longer enough.

I was experiencing what most blind people experience sooner or later. They want—but "want" isn't strong enough; "need" is a better word—they need to belong to the world around them. All of us, while apparently separate and distinct individuals, are but the molecules of which the body of humanity is composed, and each of us feels a compulsion to function as a part of the whole. Consciously or subconsciously we long to be useful and accepted, regarded with favor. Loss of sight does not change this, I discovered; I needed to find a way to belong.

What could I do? What did other blind people do? Some of them were musicians, lawyers, and journalists, but I lacked the necessary training for these professions. I understood and could perform secretarial work, but I knew that now that I was blind my chances of finding employment in a busy modern office were practically nil.

I turned to the consideration of other kinds of work done by the blind—making mops, brooms, and brushes; weaving rugs, bathmats, pot pads; simple sewing, such as pillow cases; mattress making and piano tuning. The list was long, but not one of these jobs interested me even remotely. Yet I had to have something to do. Frantically I pawed at the bottom of the trunk containing my personal resources, looking for some remnant from which I could make a future. But there was none.

Then one day Al came in with a contract for another season's work at the pier, and I was seized by a feeling of such frustration that it seemed I couldn't stand it. A contract meant summer heat, crowds, laughter, and the fun of riding, and now blindness was denying me my right to take an active part.

I strained at the leash, remembering all these things, and as I remembered I began to wonder. Was it necessary for me to give it up? After nearly eight years' experience I had a thorough understanding of my work, and surely continuing to do something which I understood would not be so difficult as trying to learn a new skill.

For two or three days I mulled over the prospect of diving off the higher tower, because I thought I would need an overwhelming array of arguments before broaching the idea to Al. When I brought it up, however, he didn't even seem surprised. He merely said I would have to get the doctor's permission before attempting any riding.

Throughout the winter we had been driving to Atlantic City every two weeks for an examination. I never knew exactly why. It was an arrangement which Al and the doctor had settled between themselves—mainly, I think, to satisfy Al that no stone had been left unturned, although it was probable also that the doctor hoped to learn something new by studying the various stages my eyes were going through. Aside from the routine examination, nothing was ever done. The nurse put some drops in my eyes to dilate the pupils, then we went to the dark room where the doctor explained that he was staring into my eyes with his little gadget. He usually concluded the examination with "Hmmmmm."

I always referred to these trips as "jic jaunts"—"just in case"—but I didn't mind them because I liked my doctor and enjoyed our informal chats with him. Apparently he had learned a thing or two about me during our months of doctor-patient relationship, and he too exhibited no surprise when I described what I wanted to do. Instead he replied that he thought it would be a wonderful thing for me both mentally and physically if I could bring it off. As matters stood, he could see no reason why I shouldn't at least try, provided I wore some sort of helmet with unbreakable lens. This sounded like locking the barn door after the horse had been stolen, but he explained that, after all, it was possible that some doctor might discover a method of treatment which might help me, provided my eyes were not subjected to any more abuse.

On our way back to Quakertown we went through Philadelphia to Spalding, the sporting goods manufacturer, about designing and making a helmet for me. The man to whom we talked promised I would have it by the middle of May, possibly a little before. This was very good timing, for it would give me an opportunity to practice in it a few times before the pier opened officially on the seventeenth. That was now only about six weeks away.

I went back to Quakertown in a completely different frame of mind. I was tremendously excited over the prospect of returning to the thing I loved best. As far as being successful at riding was concerned, the main problem would be, I knew, mounting. Once I was on, I would have nothing to worry about; then the horse would take over. There was just that all-important split second when I must mount him as he went by. If I missed I would fail completely. The idea of failure was very nearly unbearable to me, but I didn't express my fears to anyone, least of all to Al. I put my fears aside temporarily and concentrated on getting in shape.

I had not gained any weight during the winter but had lost a lot of strength, so Al hung a trap bar up in the barn for me and I began a daily routine of strenuous calisthenics and trap-bar exercises that reminded me of that first training period in Durham. Between daily sessions with the exercises and nightly sessions with a liniment bottle I managed to get in pretty good condition by the time we left for Atlantic City on May 1.

When we arrived we found that Mr. Gravitt, the new manager of the pier, had signed almost the same cast as had been there the year before. The roster included our friends Orville and Roxie LaRose and Irene Berger. We decided that this year we would all take an apartment together and get Mrs. Van Myers to do the cooking.

We wanted a place within walking distance of the pier, which wasn't easy to find for such a large group, but we finally located one that would do. It had two bedrooms and a living room, a dining room, kitchen, and bath. Al and I would have one bedroom, Roxie and Orville the other, and Irene and Arnette could fix the living room to serve as sleeping quarters.

After we got settled I spent most of my time at the pier, still working at getting my strength back. One of the performers had an extra pair of rings, and he hung them on a crossbrace underneath our tower so that I could continue my exercises. Each day I climbed the Hawaiian ladder, which was 105 feet high, and I also climbed our ramp periodically to get the feel of it. I counted the cleats as I went up. This was my method of judging how close I was to the top. I tried climbing once without holding onto the rail but found that I veered from side to side.

I had a tendency to pull to the right when walking alone, which caused me to get lost if the distance was more than fifteen or twenty feet, so Al stretched a rope from the door that provided the exit and entrance backstage to the foot of the ramp of the tower. Since this door was directly opposite my dressing room, by walking straight out I could touch it almost immediately and be guided by the rope all the way to the ramp. It wasn't necessary for me to hold onto it with my hand. The feel of the fringe of my shawl brushing it was all the guidance I needed.

Thus I managed to conceal my blindness, not out of sensitivity, as some people suspected, but out of pride and dignity. I felt that if I rode well I needed no excuse and that if I needed an excuse I had no business riding. I tried in every way possible to play down the melodramatics, refusing to allow any publicity. As far as I was concerned, when the time came for me to make my first ride the audience would not have the least idea I was blind.

With these details taken care of, costumes claimed my attention. I had some two-piece spangled suits which I wore for evening performances, and the difference in cut assured an easy selection, but the suits I wore for daytime shows were all the same style. Their only difference was in color, which of course I couldn't tell without asking someone. I solved this problem by using small buttons for identification. A button on the right shoulder marked the red suit; a button on the left shoulder, the blue one; a button on the inside of the right leg, the yellow suit, and so down the line.

Now I was ready to ride. Outwardly, anyway. Inwardly I was beginning to feel more and more turmoil as to whether I could mount the horse or not. One moment I seemed to be certain that I could; the next, that I could not. So the pendulum swung back and forth and back, though I still did not voice my fears aloud. Al must have been able to see that I was worried.

One day he said, "I don't like to be the one to bring it up, but there's something I want you to know. If it makes you feel any better, keep in mind that I wouldn't let you ride if I didn't think you could do it."

This gave me some momentary confidence as I awaited the arrival of my helmet, but on May 14, in place of the helmet, we received a letter from Spalding.

We regret to inform you that we have had difficulty with the design and will not be able to deliver it to you until about June 1.

"Oh no!" I wailed.

"Yes," Al answered. "I'm afraid so."

"But I'm all primed! I'm ready! Waiting will be bad!"

"Not any worse," he said, "than the time Daddy made you wait a week to make your first dive. And, as I recall, you did just fine."

"But this is different!" I said. "It's *very* important. It's important that I get the first time over with. After that it won't matter."

"I know," he said, "I know."

There was nothing either of us could do, however. Fortunately we had someone who could ride in my place until the helmet came. Elsa, the girl who rode for Lorena, did not have to be on the road until the first week in June. Al wired her, asking her to ride for us until then, and she wired back that she would.

Waiting was not easy—it never is—but I managed, and when May 28 rolled by, this nerve-racking period was almost over.

Seventeen

Our act was the finale of the show that year, as it had always been. The one just ahead of ours was "The Fearless Falcons," and the one before theirs the comedy horse act "Spark Plug."

The night it happened I was sitting on a bench backstage, near the wall that separated the audience from the performers, talking to Mrs. Cims, a trapeze performer, conscious at the same time that the music being played out front was "Barney Google with Those Goo-Goo-Googly Eyes." Sparkey and Kelsey must be waltzing, I thought, because the audience was roaring with laughter. Soon they would make their ridiculous bow with all four legs going different ways and go running offstage at a crazy gallop.

We continued talking for a short while, and then Mrs. Cims left. As she did so the Barney Google music ended and there was a big hand for Sparkey and Kelsey. As soon as the clapping died away the music for "The Fearless Falcons" began, and I knew that Roxie and Irene and Orville were going on. Theirs was about a twenty-minute act. Soon Elsa, who was going to ride Klatawah, would be coming from the dressing room on her way to the ramp, and since I had something I wanted to talk to her about I walked over to the guide rope Al had rigged up for me and leaned against the wall, waiting for her to pass.

As I stood there listening to the music, I could follow the progress of the Falcons out front. I had watched them so often in previous years that I knew almost to the instant what they were doing. Orville would be working from the cradle between the two poles holding the trap bar and rings for the girls to perform on. His feet would be hooked between the two parallel bars of supple metal that ran from one perch pole to the other, and from these bars he would be hanging head down, flexing, unflexing, doing a few tricks while the girls climbed the ladders up to him.

Both girls' lives depended on him completely, for if he ever lost his grip on the trapeze or the rings they would plunge down onto the deck 104 feet below. They worked without a net, because if they fell from that height the fall would kill them anyway.

After a few minutes the sweep of "The Skater's Waltz" swung onto the night air and I pictured Roxie in trap-bar routine. She had several tricks—a bird's nest, a foot-and-hand change, and a split in the rings. After each of these the audience clapped, and then there was heavy applause and I knew she had stepped back onto her pedestal, giving Irene a chance to perform.

Up until the past week Irene had been doing an especially complicated foot-and-hand change, which is difficult to describe but so dangerous that Orville had cut it out of the act. The danger lay in the fact that for a split second she was completely free of contact with anything at all, and if in coming from the poles to the rings she didn't catch hold of Orville's hand she would fall free. Irene loved that particular routine because she loved flirting with death. When Orville forbade her doing it any more she threatened to quit but finally settled for a belly roll, which got more screams from the crowd anyway because it appeared more dramatic. The foot-and-hand change was too subtle and too quick for most people to follow.

The belly roll was performed on the trap bar and was a real chiller. Irene would put her stomach on the bar, swing back and forth on it a minute, and then fling herself forward and scream. As she shot down she would appear to have lost control, but at the last minute she would catch herself with her feet and hang swinging head down. When I heard "Springtime in the Rockies" I knew Irene had begun and that she would soon have the audience standing up in their seats.

I smiled to myself as I stood against the wall, still waiting for Elsa to come. The audience exhaled their usual gasps and "Ohhhs" and "Ahhhs," signaling the end of that part of the act. Now while the girls climbed to the top of the perch poles, Orville would descend, ready to help the four men who paid out the rope which brought the girls down to the ground at the end of the performance.

In my mind's eye I could see Irene and Roxie as they climbed, their little bodies moving upward, one a bright flash of silver, the other a heavy glitter of gold. Swiftly as twin spiders they would climb up and up until they reached the top, 125 feet in the air. There they would pause to wave to the crowd below, and as they did so the little bits of glitter they wore in their hair would catch in the spotlights and wink down at the crowd. Then they would fasten their feet into the slings and begin their gymnastics, swaying back and forth on the poles, half flinging themselves out and up and down and with their exertions bending the poles to almost forty-five-degree angles.

This part of the act usually took about ten minutes, and during that time, except for occasional gasps, one could hear a pin drop. Every face, I knew, was glued to the girls on the poles and a good many mouths had dropped open. Then the brazenly jubilant strains of "The Stars and Stripes Forever" broke on the night air; the act was finished and the girls were coming down.

The audience burst into wild applause. I had a clear mental picture of the two girls: Roxie, with her auburn hair tossed back, clamping her teeth tight on the rubber bit in her mouth, arms flung behind her body like some beautiful silver bird; Irene, above her on the same rope, frozen in an arabesque, a golden butterfly, her body forward, one leg thrust out in a graceful arc. Then suddenly there was a terrible scream, not from one throat, but from eight thousand.

I was accustomed to hearing the audience scream when the girls did their tricks, but this was different. It was long and drawn out and laden with terror. I turned cold at the mass scream, and almost simultaneously there was the sound of a dull thud on the deck outside. It made me physically ill.

Behind and a little to the left of me a dice game had been in progress, and I was dimly aware of incoherent, animal-like noises from the players as they scrambled to their feet. Above the seemingly endless sounds of screaming I heard the slow creaking and grinding of metal, as if it were being twisted and bent. Then another heavy thud. I waited with a feeling of terrible suspense for the sound of a third body, forgetting momentarily that Orville was already down.

Behind me I heard Harriet, one of the Hawaiian divers, shouting and realized, as in a dream, that she was shouting at me. In the confusion of that whole dreadful moment my ears registered her warning but not her words.

Responding to them, I turned and ran a few steps and bumped into a bench. I did not fall completely over it but I did fall forward. The thundering crash of metal breaking and wood splintering seemed very close, and then there was a final crash.

Almost immediately someone grabbed my arm and rushed me across the area to my dressing room. "Stay here," he said. "You'll be safe." As he spoke and pushed me inside I knew that it was Marty.

The sound of shouting voices and running feet was rising tumultuously as he opened the weatherproof telephone box that hung on the wall outside my door and called frantically for an ambulance.

Roxie was the first to be brought backstage, though she was the second to fall. This was because PeeWee, the first person to reach Irene, had started toward the front of the pier with her in his arms. Somebody caught him and headed him backstage, but Roxie had been carried there in the meantime and was put on the only cot in the first-aid room. Between cries of pain I could hear her say, "My back! Oh, God! My back!" and then, as if she had lapsed into a partial state of consciousness and with less agony in her voice, "What's the matter? Is something wrong? What's happened?"

PeeWee finally arrived with Irene and laid her on a bench outside my door. In contrast to Roxie, Irene was silent, too silent. I wondered which was worse—Roxie's cries so full of pain or Irene's silence. Then someone said, "Here's a nurse. She was in the audience," and someone else said, "Where's Mrs. Pallenberg? Tell her to take care of Emile. He's sick."

A new voice, a woman's, spoke after a minute and said, "I can't do anything for this one," and then I heard her going into the first-aid room to see about Roxie.

Little Dirbima Pallenberg seemed to be wandering around lost. "Is somebody dead?" she was asking. "Did somebody get killed?" and I thought, "Why doesn't somebody take the child away from this?" I opened my door and called, "Dirbima, come here," but just then Mr. Pallenberg spoke up. "Never mind," he said, "there isn't anything I can do, so I'm taking her home."

I closed the door again, but it was opened immediately by Harriet. She was crying as she entered, "Oh, I'm so glad, so glad!" For an instant I felt shocked and then thought, "She's hysterical. She doesn't know what she's saying."

I said, "Tell me what happened, Harriet," and she began, "Irene—she—" But her voice broke and she began sobbing more violently. I made no effort to comfort her. I had no words.

I remained at the door, wondering why the ambulance was taking so long. Outside I could hear Orville speaking—crying, really. He was saying, "I'm through. I'll never build another rigging as long as I live." I felt vaguely surprised that he wasn't hurt, until I remembered that he had been on the deck at the time of the accident rather than in the cradle. Then somebody shouted, "Here come the stretcher-bearers."

A few seconds later Al dashed in, kissed me, and said, "I'm going to the hospital with Orville. When Arnette gets dressed, go on home."

Harriet got up and went out, and in a minute I followed her. I moved toward a group of voices, and as I did so Pee-Wee stepped up and placed his hands on my shoulders. "Thank God," he said, "you're still with us."

It seemed such an odd thing for him to say that I asked, "What in the world do you mean?"

"If it hadn't been for that bench," he said, "you'd have been killed. The rigging crashed down less than a foot above your head as you fell." Listening to the story of my close call, I understood for the first time what Harriet had meant when she said, "Oh, I'm so glad."

The theory that the show must go on was ignored by the spectators, making it totally unnecessary to call it off. Many of the spectators had fainted, but those who were able to left the grandstand, and as Arnette and I passed by on our way out it was deserted, she reported, except for a few who had not yet recovered, their friends and the ushers who were helping to revive them.

As we walked along the corridors of the pier, usually so thronged with pleasure seekers, it was strangely empty, and the few late-comers who had bought tickets after the accident wandered about seemingly bewildered and lost. At the front end of the pier somebody told us that the horror of the spectators who had seen the accident had been translated to those who had not, and crowds had left the pier like refugees pouring from a doomed city.

Some of the performers went home, but others, anxious for news and knowing Al would bring it when he came, followed us to our apartment. We gathered in the dining room and sat down around the table, miserably unhappy.

The differences in the characters of the individuals were revealed by their reactions. Those who felt compelled to talk discussed the accident in all its phases, and as I listened I gradually gained an idea of what had happened. Apparently Harriet had been the only one who was watching. "When Irene got on the rope," she explained, "instead of spreading out into the arabesque, it looked as if she went into a back bend."

The instant she said it I remembered hearing Irene talk about a back bend. She said she was tired of the arabesque and wanted to try something different. It was conceivable that she had decided on the spur of the moment to do it without having first figured out that she would have to wrap her leg around the rope in a manner directly opposite from the pose required by an arabesque. When she pushed back with her weight instead of forward, the rope would have come unwrapped from around her leg and she would have fallen. That was and still is the best theory any of us has been able to offer. No explanation of the accident really makes sense, because Irene was such a marvelous performer, but it seems unlikely that it could have happened any other way.

As Irene fell she struck two wires, one at sixty feet and another at fifty, which caused the anchor hooks to straighten out. This sudden and forceful release of the two supporting guy wires on the same side that held Roxie's weight was too much of a strain, and the rigging collapsed. The men couldn't pay the rope out fast enough to let Roxie down easy, so she had fallen from about seventy-five feet. Marty said that when he got to her he found one of the bones in her ankle had broken through the flesh and was sticking into the planking of the deck. He and the others who lifted her had to pull the bone out of the wood and in the process broke part of it off.

After Marty's description everybody was silent for a while, and then Kelsey began talking about other accidents and continued for some time in this vein, piling up harrowing and gruesome details. Finally someone threatened to throw him out if he didn't shut up, and the threat was backed up by a chorus of "Yes, for heaven's sake!" Then there was another silence.

Finally Al came home about four o'clock in the morning and told us that Irene was dead. The surgeons believed she had broken her back when she hit the first guy wire and her neck when she hit the second one. She never regained consciousness, but her vitality had been so great that she had lived for nearly two hours. Roxie's injuries were compound and still not definitely catalogued. She had a badly fractured ankle and a broken foot. Several vertebrae in the lower part of her spine had been crushed, and the doctors didn't know whether she would live or not.

Finally we went to bed, and I fell asleep almost instantly, taking refuge in the only place where I could keep from thinking.

When I woke about nine the next morning I felt drugged, and as I struggled to overcome the sensation I became conscious of a sense of guilt, and the atmosphere seemed heavy with vague desolation. I couldn't think why at first, and then I remembered; Irene was dead and Roxie was in the hospital. She too might be dying or dead by now. But it was impossible! It was just a bad dream. In a few minutes we would all get up and have breakfast together.

I opened my eyes, and the simple act brought with it the realization that it was all true. I got up, slipped on a robe, and went out into the hall. Arnette met me and said, "Al has gone to the hospital. Mrs. Van Myers is here." Her voice was dull and even, and I felt she had spoken less for the purpose of giving information than to appear balanced and in control of her emotions.

In a little while Al came back with Orville and made him go to bed. Roxie's life was still hanging by a hair, Al said. We tried to eat breakfast, but it was no use; empty chairs around the table were as visible to me in my mind's eye as they were to Al and Arnette. We gave up and went down to the pier.

The wreckage had been cleared away, and many who had been too stunned to weep the night before were weeping openly now. Arnette expressed the feelings of us all when she said, "It's hard to tell whether it would be worse looking at all the wrecked rigging or the empty space where it stood. It's horrible, that wide empty place on the deck."

During the next few days Roxie fought for her life and Orville was seldom at the apartment. Orville's mother arrived from Des Moines in time to attend Irene's funeral. She hadn't known Irene, but her presence comforted Orville. Of course the whole thing was worse for him than for anyone else, but the aftermath of the tragedy had its effect on all of us.

During the next few days everything seemed to go wrong, from minor injuries to major ones, and odd, uncalculated happenings took place. Perez, a slackwire performer, fell and injured a foot, and one of the girls in the water sports fell off her aquaplane as it made a turn, and the board flipped up and laid her head open. Worst of all, at the end of the week one of the Pallenberg bears got loose and mangled Tommy Kao.

Tommy had been taking a sun bath and fallen asleep while the Pallenberg act was on. The bear got off his leash somehow and darted backstage through the half-open door. The shouts of the crowd excited him even more, and as he ran back he found Tommy lying on the bench and attacked him.

My first impulse when I heard the commotion outside was to open the screen door of my dressing room to let some of the scattering performers find safety inside, but the instinct toward self-preservation squelched the impulse quickly. A wide-open door might prove an invitation to the bear, and so I stood there anxiously wondering if I should change my mind and be brave. Then I heard high-pitched screams like those of a woman in pain and immediately thought of Arnette. I opened the door and started out, propelled forward by my fear for her safety, which was suddenly greater than my fear for myself. But just then I heard a scuffling sound and stopped as Mr. Wylie, owner of the aero-wheel act, called out, "Somebody help Tommy while I take care of this bear," and I realized it was Tommy who had cried out. This was followed by a breaking and splintering noise. Mr. Pallenberg mumbled something. A few minutes later he had the bear under control and back on his chain.

Tommy's injuries proved minor—a clawed back and chewed hand, both of which would heal—but tempers were running so high and everyone was under such a strain that Mr. Pallenberg later had a fight with Mr. Wylie because Mr. Wylie had hit the talented animal with a chain. Reports from eyewitnesses stated that after Mr. Wylie hit him over the head the bear had worn a definitely woozy expression.

These were the outward aftereffects of the tragedy. The inward effects were less visible, but all of us were scarred to some degree. Everything considered, I felt I had more reason than any of the others to be affected by Irene's death and Roxie's desperate injuries, for I was about to face the ordeal of riding *blind*. My helmet had just arrived and Elsa was scheduled to leave in three days; soon I would make my first ride.

It was hard to think of Irene and Roxie and not be haunted by doubts. It seemed foolish, presumptuous even, for me to think I could do my act without injury when performers who had sight were being injured daily. Again the pendulum swung from doubt to certainty to doubt. Could I do it? Of course I could. How did I know?

It is debatable how long these inner arguments would have continued had it not been that they were all reconciled suddenly by a circumstance no one had foreseen.

Eighteen

I was scheduled to make my first ride on the seventh. On the third, Elsa, who had just finished the last afternoon performance, was in my dressing room changing when she received a telegram from Lorena. Lorena's season had not been due to open until the tenth, or so she thought. However, the message said that she had gotten her dates confused and the park was opening the night of the fourth. This meant that Elsa would have time to do nothing more than throw her belongings into a trunk and leave.

I heard this news with a mixture of panic and relief. My first thought was, "Oh no!" but my second was, "The waiting is over."

I had planned to make a practice dive before Elsa left, but now that was impossible. With only about an hour between the last afternoon performance and the one of the evening, I would hardly have time to do more than get my things together and get dressed before I would have to be ready to go on. I made my preparations automatically and had almost finished when Al came along.

"Are you up to this?" he asked the minute he walked in.

I said, "I think so."

"If you're not," he proposed, "you know we can call it off. I'm sure Mr. Gravitt would understand."

"Yes, I know."

There was silence for a moment. Then I added, "I've got to do it."

He said, "Yes, I think you must.... Will you let me come up with you? Just this first time to stop the horse? I can hold him while you get on. That's all that's really worrying you."

"No," I replied, "I'd rather you didn't. I've got to do it alone."

He was quiet a minute. Then he asked, "Are you afraid?"

"I don't know," I said. "I don't think so. I haven't had time to think."

"It's better," he said, "if you don't think. Just go up there like it was old times and keep remembering how often you've done it."

"All right, I will."

He looked at his watch. 'It's almost seven. I have to leave."

"All right," I repeated. "And don't worry."

He kissed me and, a moment afterward, left

I picked up the helmet, testing the feel and the weight, hefting it in my hand. Although a football helmet, it was much heavier and clumsier than standard models because of the metal frame on the front which encased a piece of clear plastic. The plastic came down over my eyes and fitted across my nose. The back of the helmet laced up so that I could adjust it to my head, and the inside was padded with foam rubber. To hold it on there was a strap with a buckle that fastened beneath my chin. After I had tried it on several times I threw my shawl around my shoulders and went out.

On the bench outside my door where I had often waited in the past I sat now, feeling the raw spring breeze nip at me. I wished it were a warm night; somehow that would have been better, but it wasn't a warm night and that's all there was to it.

I followed the music out front, checking off each act in turn, and after a while I heard Dempsey coming down the pier. He was barking furiously, making way for Red Lips, and in a moment George and the horse came around the comer and halted at the foot of the ramp.

Sparkey and Kelsey were about through. I would be on next. I got up and crossed over to the guide rope and let the fringe of my shawl brush it as I walked to the foot of the ramp. The applause out front ended for "Spark Plug," and Al began our announcement.

"Ladies and gentlemen, you are about to witness the most exciting act in show business today. All eyes cast atop this lof-ty tower—"

I turned and put my shawl on the railing and buckled on my helmet. Then I began to climb.

As I mounted I counted the cleats. I already knew how many there were, but if I counted it would keep my mind off other things. I began dutifully, "One . . . two . . . three . . . four," thinking how familiar they felt, "five ... six ... seven ... eight," and how I must do as Al said. "Nine ... ten . . . eleven ... twelve." But the fear was creeping up. Would I be able to mount Red? Would I be able to tell where he was? Moving sound was hard to pinpoint. My actions would have to be precise. A split second off and I'd miss him. I could lose my balance and fall. "Twenty-five ... twenty-six ... twenty-seven." I had lost track and was counting at random. "Twenty-eight... twenty-nine .. . thirty." As I continued I felt like yawning and remembered an article I had read. Yawning, it said, was caused by three things: boredom, illness, or fear. "Forty-one . . . forty-two . . . forty-three . . ." Roxie was badly crippled. She would live. When she learned she might have to lie in bed for the rest of her life would she still want to? Would I be like Roxie? Could that happen to me? Yes, it could and I know it could. "Seventy-five ... seventy-six ... seventy-seven ..." Just as I started to say "Seventy-nine" my foot came down with a thump, the kind of thump that follows an attempt to take a step where there isn't any. I knew I had reached the level floor of the platform. As I stepped forward I heard Al say, "And now, ladies and gentlemen, Miss Sonora and Red Lips."

In the old days I always tried to time my arrival at the top with his concluding words and had been pleased when we synchronized. Tonight I had done it without trying and thought, "That's a good omen!" But almost immediately the feeling of well-being was dispelled, for as I boosted myself up on the railing and listened for the sound of George turning Red Lips, I could not hear a thing from the bottom of the ramp!

For a split second I thought I had lost my hearing, and panic seized me. Then I detected hoofs on the ramp and felt their vibration. Thank Cod! I could hear him, though not as clearly as I had expected.

I realized that the foam rubber inside the helmet partially deadened sound. Still, I would be able to hear him better the closer he got, and I tensed on the railing, remembering how fast Red traveled. Then, when pounding feet and vibration told me he was very close, I held out my hand and felt the tip of an ear flick by my fingers. Immediately I lowered my hand; I had reached too high. I found the side of his neck and felt the coarse hair of his body brush by. The next instant I closed my hand over the neck strap and threw my leg over Red's back. In one swift motion I mounted him and knew I had mounted him perfectly!

A shaft of joy shot through me that was akin to pain as I pressed my legs against him tightly out of sheer animal pleasure. The firmness of his flesh, of his muscles, the contours of his body—all these fit into my own as naturally as if they were part of me, and I had the feeling that I had suddenly been made whole. It was as if I had lost an arm or a leg and gotten it back again. It was as if I had found a part of myself I had never hoped to regain.

Red was at the head of the platform doing his little dance, first one foot and then the other drumming on the platform; then he slid down over the edge and hung there for a second. He slammed his forefeet against the panel with terrific force and launched us out into space. Once again I had that feeling of wild exhilaration as we were heading down, down, down, toward the tank of water. I felt the rippling of his muscles as the horse prepared to enter, and as he straightened his forelegs I tightened my grip on the harness. The next instant we hit the water in a perfect dive.

The water gurgled and bubbled; his forefeet touched bottom. He threw his head back and sprang upward toward the surface, springing with such power that when he came in view of the audience he shot halfway out of the water. I clung to his wet and slippery back as his feet pawed the air. He settled back in the water and began to swim to the incline. In a moment we came out at a brisk canter, and I slid off his back. I found Al waiting for me and he said, "I think you're wonderful."

The audience seemed to be applauding as they had never applauded before. They could not have known and yet seemed to know that something special had happened. Al handed me Red Lips' sugar and I put it between

156

my lips. For some time before I lost my sight we had been training him to take it from me in this fashion so that it appeared he was kissing me. Red leaned over and took it, and the audience clapped harder. This time it went on and on until it became an ovation.

It followed me as I left the stage and made my way to my dressing room. Backstage the other performers rushed up to me. Everyone kissed and hugged me, and as I went into my dressing room I felt wonderfully warm.

I walked over to the mirror that hung on a wall and stood a minute before it. It was the same mirror I had looked into eight years before on the night I made my first ride. I had seen myself then literally bursting with joy, a smile on my face like no other. I couldn't see the smile now but I knew it was there and, best of all, in place of the lonely victory I had had that night I now had friends to share my happiness. It seemed to me that in some odd way a balance had been struck.

That was the beginning of eleven years during which I rode blind. Not all the dives went as smoothly as the first one; I had some close scrapes. Sometimes I became overanxious about mounting the horse and jumped on him the moment my hand touched his body instead of taking time to find the harness. When this happened I landed halfway between his head and withers—a very unhandy place—from which I had to move back quickly to get into proper position before he dived.

Other times a poor mount would make me lose my grip and I would get knocked off when he hit the water. Since I could not see, this was especially dangerous. When I had sight I used to wait in the bottom of the tank until the horse began to swim out, but now I had no way of locating him. Being knocked off caused me some consternation, for I was afraid I might come up directly under him and get caught in the mad thrash of his hoofs. Fortunately it didn't happen often enough for the odds to stack up against me, and I never did get kicked, though one day perhaps I deserved to be.

I had oiled myself and put on an old bathing suit and gone outside to take a sun bath until time for my performance. I hadn't intended to take a nap, but the warm sun made me drowsy, and the next thing I knew someone was shaking me and saying it was almost time. I had only a few minutes to run to my dressing room and change. I managed to get dressed in the nick of time and made my way up the ramp, but it was not until I was on the tower and the horse was approaching that I remembered the oil on my body. I knew I was liable to slip off him, and to overcome this possibility I exerted an even tighter grip than usual as we took off, but it was no use. The minute we hit the water I felt myself going, but this time the sensation was one of slipping rather than being knocked off.

As I lost my grip I could feel the horse's body beneath me and made a desperate effort to regain my hold on the harness as he continued forward and down. My clutching fingers raked along his back and over his rump and then onto his tail. I knew this was my last chance, so I closed my hands on it and hung on, straightening my body to avoid his thrashing hoofs. When we reached the surface I gave my body a tremendous yank, which sent me forward in a gliding, surfboard manner, and got hold of the harness. I pulled myself into position and rode out, very pleased.

Another time—four times, in fact!—I missed the horse entirely. I misjudged the sound of his clattering hoofs and failed to mount him as he passed. Once when this happened in Superior, Wisconsin, it made me so angry to be left sitting on the rail like a flowerpot on a window sill that I decided I would do something about it.

Ordinarily Red took off whether I was on him or not, but that night he seemed to be waiting for me, so, clinging to the railing, I moved forward until his body blocked my advance; then I climbed up and extended my right foot to the railing on the other side and stood up. I was poised above him like a Colossus. I heard Al shout. "Don't do it! Don't do it!" but ignored his warning.

I started inching my way forward once more. When I got to the front of the tower I reached down, felt for the harness, and dropped into position—at the last possible moment before Red took off.

Mishaps didn't take place often, but whenever they did Al threatened to make me quit riding. I always managed to talk him out of it and in all those eleven years never experienced any injury more serious than a sprained ankle.

I rode for five years before I changed my policy about no publicity regarding my blindness. Once when we were appearing at Charlotte, North Carolina, a reporter from one of the newspapers came to interview me. While he was there another reporter, who had visited me the day before, came in. "Say," he said, "somebody just told me that you can't see. I came over to ask you personally because I don't believe it."

"Yes, it's true."

"Well, I want to shake your hand," he said, "because I think you're the most remarkable person I've ever met."

The first reporter contributed, "Well, I've been talking to her for twenty minutes and I didn't know she couldn't see."

After the handshaker had gone I realized from the trend of the remaining reporter's questions that he was planning to make my handicap the main theme of his interview, so I hurriedly told him that I frowned on such publicity and explained my reasons for doing so. He seemed willing to let the matter rest and we continued our conversation along other lines, but a few minutes later he mentioned my blindness again. His persuasive arguments for permission to write it up finally won my consent.

The interview appeared in the next day's paper, and shortly thereafter I had a visitor. He was a minister who explained that the story had aroused his interest because he was on a committee in charge of raising money for a training school and factory for the blind of Charlotte. He wanted me to appear on a local radio station to make an appeal for funds. It was a request I could not refuse, nor did I wish to do so. The story in the newspaper and the radio interview attracted enough attention to set wheels in motion, and one morning I awoke to find a syndicated feature, a biography with pictures of myself, spread over half a page of a chain of newspapers.

At first I was genuinely annoyed at this publicity; then letters began to come in—not just a few but dozens—from people all over the country. They wrote to say in one way or another how much the story had meant to them and how it had inspired them to go on living as normally as possible in spite of their particular handicaps. This response forced me to scrutinize more closely my original ideas about personal publicity. I came to the conclusion that if knowledge of my blindness in combination with my success as a rider could help others, then it was both rude and selfish of me to keep it a secret. After that I never tried.

In 1942 we opened in what proved to be our last engagement. America had been in the war only a few months, but we had trouble getting men to excavate the tank, carpenters and laborers to set up the tower, and a groom to take care of Red Lips. (Our current groom had given up horses for army trucks.) Furthermore, by the time we completed our contracted appearance at Playland Park in Houston, Texas, there were rigid restrictions on tires and gasoline, and many fair associations were canceling their annual fairs for the duration. We decided the time to quit had come. We would put Red Lips out to pasture and take to the pasture ourselves.

I was ready, but Al was not. Al was and is a real showman, and real showmen love the business as they love nothing else in the world. They not only love it but need it with an inner craving and are miserable away from the noise and excitement of fairgrounds and amusement parks. In my years of show business I had found this to be true to the lowest-paid roustabout as well as the managers and star performers. Once a man had been truly smitten by show business, he was never free of its lure.

When I had my sight I often watched the roustabouts strike the tents or put them up and was impressed by the enthusiasm with which they worked. One would have thought they were going to be paid a thousand dollars, while the truth of the matter was they earned far less than men of similar skills on a routine construction job. They worked without flagging in sleet and rain. I have seen them, after they finished, wrap themselves up in an old tarpaulin, huddle beneath a wagon, and fall sound asleep, as content to be there as they would have been nowhere else in the world.

Few of them ever left show business for anything else. They seldom wrote or went home or even claimed to have a home. Once I asked a man who was working for us whom I should notify if he got hurt, and he said, "Lady, if anything happens to me, just throw me in that horse tank and pile on the dirt."

Al was like the roustabouts. Show business was his life, and when he had to leave it, it nearly broke his heart. He would go back now if he were able, but physically he is not. He works as a motel desk clerk at night, and I work during the day as a typist at the Lighthouse for the Blind. Because of our working hours we don't see as much of each other as we'd like, but before he has to leave in the evening we have our dinner together. He fills me in on what has happened during the day, or I tell him what's going on at the office, or we talk about the old days and performers we have known. When he's feeling especially nostalgic, he tells me stories about his days with the circus.

Sometimes old friends visit us, but mostly we live by ourselves, hearing infrequently from people we knew in Atlantic City. We haven't seen Orville and Roxie for a long time, but we learned that Roxie was able to get out of bed after two years and walk on crutches. After a while she managed to hobble around on her own, though with a very bad limp. She was never able to perform again, which was very sad. She had been such a wonderful acrobat—and such a beautiful girl.

Arnette and I are still close, though a thousand and more miles apart. She and her husband and two children live in Pennsylvania, where she makes a constant effort, she says, to keep house better than Mother did.

Red Lips died in 1954. We had left him in Houston with friends. All the other horses were long since dead—Klatawah, Snow, and John. When I think of them and our years together I feel some of Al's nostalgia, but I remind myself that We promises many new experiences.

I often have the feeling that I am part of the world and, though I cannot see my surroundings, the world is part of me. I am conscious of an indestructible, indomitable force, a constant and abiding truth that is stronger than any human being. This presence gives me strength and courage to face whatever comes, and I do not fear life or anything in it. On the contrary, I relish life and know that there is still much for me to do and to know.